W9-CMS-865

Japanese
Quilts

Iku Hara is over eighty years old, and she keeps herself busy making patchwork quilts and *futon* covers. "I teach calligraphy," she tells us, "but patchwork is the hobby I enjoy most. I like designing and combining colors, of course, but I am really the sort of person who enjoys the process more than the result." She is seen here with her traditional sewing box and ironing board on the floor beside her. Japanese dressmakers use a pincushion fixed to a stand. Photograph courtesy Rieko Ariyoshi.

Japanese Quilts

Jill Liddell
& Yuko Watanabe

E. P. DUTTON NEW YORK

A Note About the Detail Photographs

Page v: Detail from *Memories of Japan* (1985) by Adrienne Westmore, Falls Church, Virginia. The complete quilt is illustrated on page 128.

Page vi: Detail showing an example of Hisako Sakamoto's "Fabric Calligraphy" in process. The brightly colored character in this illustration means "joy." Sakamoto is from Tokyo, and her piece called *Iroha Characters* (1985) is illustrated on page 51.

Page viii: Detail from *A Maze* (1984) by Ritsuko Takahashi, Tokyo. The complete quilt is illustrated on page 83.

Book design by Nancy Danahy

Published in the United States by E. P. Dutton, a division of NAL Penguin Inc., 2 Park Avenue, New York, N.Y. 10016. / Published simultaneously in Canada by Fitzhenry and Whiteside Limited, Toronto. / Library of Congress Catalog Card Number: 88-71760. / Printed and bound by Dai Nippon Printing Co., Ltd., Tokyo, Japan. / ISBN: 0-525-24661-4 (cloth); ISBN: 0-525-48386-1 (DP).
10 9 8 7 6 5 4 3 2 1 First Edition

We dedicate this book to Jill's mother, Susan,
and to Yuko's husband, Wanchai,
with our love.

Unless otherwise indicated by the credit lines,
all of the color plates in this book are reproduced
by gracious permission of the magazine
Patchwork Quilt Tsūshin of Tokyo, Japan,
in which they were first published.

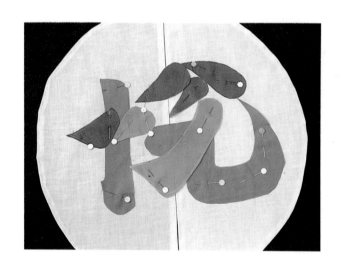

Contents

Introduction

In Japan, up until a few years ago, women happily stitched away at their quilting hoops with never a thought that their quilts were unusual until a lady Marco Polo found her way here and told us otherwise.

The passion for quiltmaking transmitted to this Far Eastern island nation came to us, of course, from America, as has been the case with most "in" things since the end of World War II. We had no idea that our quilting was no longer looking American until I met this lady Marco Polo and heard with amazement that she thought Japanese quilts were quite original.

As the editor of *Patchwork Quilt Tsūshin*, one of Japan's leading quilt magazines, I headed off to America to see the world of quilts there, and I discovered at the International Quilt Festival in Houston in 1985, and again in 1986 and 1987, that our work really was different. I also was delighted to learn that there was a growing enthusiasm in the United States for Japanese fabrics and for our own form of quilting, called *sashiko*.

This lady Marco Polo made it quite plain that Japanese quilts are worked in rich and unusual fabrics, in strange color combinations, and usually are of a simple but often asymmetrically distorted design. "Quilts from the other side of the looking-glass," she called them. Jill Liddell, my coauthor, is, of course, the lady Marco Polo, for she has been traveling for thirty years and had lived in many different countries before she came to Japan. We met, appropriately enough, at a quilting bee. We found that we had a lot in common—we are both journalists for one thing, one Eastern, one Western, and living in a common quilting world—so we decided to write a book about Japanese quilts together.

The exhibition that lit the fire of quiltmaking in the hearts of so many women inside and outside of the United States was the magnificent collection of antique quilts belonging to Jonathan Holstein and Gail Van Der Hoof. This exhibition, "Abstract Art in American Quilts," toured Japan in 1976 and really caught the imagination of Japanese women. The fifties and sixties had been uncreative years for needlewomen—handmade goods had been out of fashion—so housewives were itching to use their hands again, and although they were impressed by the wonderful graphic designs in the Holstein collection, it was also the lovely old fabrics and the use of scraps that attracted them. These old quilts made from recycled fabrics reminded Japanese needlewomen of the past, of the days when their mothers patched clothing or made household items from scraps. It didn't matter that these quilts had tears or worn patches in them, this was part of their charm. We Japanese have traditionally cherished old fabrics, and the idea of creating something artistic and useful from scraps appealed to our ideal of beauty. The Holstein exhibition stirred a memory of a way of life that had seemed destined to be lost forever.

So Japanese women took up their needles and started to reproduce what they had seen. Boxes of treasured fragments of cloth that had lain forgotten in attics and storehouses were now brought to light again, and even after it was realized that there were such things as quilts made from new fabric, the custom of recycling became one of our quiltmaking traditions. So many quilts illustrated in this book have been made from old textiles: scraps, *futon* covers, kimono, and decorative wrapping cloths like the *furoshiki* that we carry instead of a paper shopping bag.

Patchwork was not unknown in Japan, as you will see in the introductory essay "Threads of History," and American patchwork had been taught by missionaries in the country districts in the early years of this century. But many women started by using the English method of piecing over paper because this seemed the only logical way to cope with all those different-shaped patches. As interest grew and as instruction books and articles began to be translated, women formed groups, many of them centered around a quilter who had learned the craft while living in the United States. Then patchwork schools opened, and because of our craft tradition where an apprenticeship always lasts for years, an average beginner's course was scheduled to last forty weeks! But there were some quilters living in isolated country districts who did beautiful work without having ever actually seen, or felt, a genuine quilt, and they are among our most respected quiltmakers today. You will see some of their latest work in this book.

The quilt world is changing all the time here in Japan. Last year the first nationwide guild started, the Japan Quilters Association, which now has three hundred members, many of them small groups that are finding it stimulating to exchange patterns and ideas through the monthly newsletter. There are many fabric shops; Japanese quiltmakers are blessed with a ready supply of 100 percent good-quality cotton, and new quilt shops are constantly opening up all over the country. All these guilds, groups, shops, kitchen-table classes, and quilting bees have pushed Japan to the position of being the second-largest quilt market in the world.

In preparing this book, we have been given a lot of help so there are many people to whom we owe our thanks: Hiroshi Kimura, the publisher of *Patchwork Quilt Tsūshin*, for letting us reproduce so many of the photographs that first appeared in the magazine, and of course, the quilt artists, for letting us feature their beautiful work. We have also included a few quilts made by Westerners because we felt their quilts illustrated some aspect of Japanese design; thus we thank them for sending us their photographs. Thanks must also go to our editor, Cyril I. Nelson, whose enthusiasm kept the project moving and also for recommending some Japanese-made quilts that he found in New York City for us to include.

A big vote of thanks must go to my friends and helpers at *Patchwork Quilt Tsūshin:* Junko Misawa, Masako Sakurai, Masayo Hagiwara, Kumi Maekawa, Shoko Takeda, and Yoko Takeuchi, all of whom worked so hard for us, and also to Sueko Murata for help in getting photographs for the section called "Threads of History" and for modeling for us. We would particularly like to thank those people who were kind enough to assist us with information about the history of patchwork in Japan: notably Iwao Nagasaki, Assistant Curator of the Applied Arts Department of the Tokyo National Museum; Professor Ochanomizu of the Women's National University, Tokyo; Mitake Katsube, editor of the complete works of Katsu Kaishu, published by Keiso Shobo, Tokyo; Kasuko Kawada; Kayoko Muramatsu; and above all, Yoshimasa Katsu and Sumiko Gomi for their help in obtaining photographs of the *yosegire* screen for us. We owe thanks to Sachiko Shimomura of the Japan Quilters Association and, finally, to Patricia Westmacott for kindly typing the manuscript for us.

YUKO WATANABE

NOTE

When citing the names of our contemporaries, we have followed Western style in presenting the given name first and the family name last (although this is not the style used in Japan). In the historical section, the names are presented in the reverse order.

The dimensions of the quilts were given to us in centimeters, so these measurements have been rounded up or down to the nearest inch so as to avoid awkward fractions. The measurement in centimeters is, therefore, the exact one. In the measurements, height always precedes width.

Threads of History

Although quiltmaking in Japan is a comparatively new phenomenon, particularly in its current burst of popularity, all the elements—quilting, patchwork, and appliqué—have been present in this part of the world for centuries. While this book is about modern Japanese quiltmaking, it is worth examining its background in northern Asia because any fragments of history help to add to our store of knowledge about the origins of the craft, and of course, it also sheds some light on what is happening in Japan today.

The quilting of materials, that is, the concept of joining together layers of cloth with a padding in between—the basic "textile sandwich"—seems to be widely spread in those parts of the world that have cool climates; a simple and yet efficient technology against the cold. The Japanese, as is well known (and viewed with some trepidation by newcomers to the country), traditionally sleep on a channel-quilted, stab-stitched, or tied quilt laid on the floor, called a *futon*, and they pull another quilt over themselves.

Today, the top *futon* is encased in an easily washable slipcover, but in the past the *futons* were made and decorated as beautifully as money would allow: in costly woven or embroidered silks for the rich, or more modestly in indigo-dyed cottons for ordinary folk. The magnificent kimono-shaped *futon* in figure 1 is a country piece, but it was made at a time when there was prosperity in the rural areas, around the turn of the century. The thick white cotton basting threads are there to hold the three layers together, and the fact that these are visible seems not to have mattered. You will find similar basting on fine hand-painted or embroidered ceremonial wrapping cloths for gifts. With this background of padded and decorative *futons* it is no wonder that the Japanese took to American quiltmaking with such enthusiasm.

It is interesting that a type of padded *futon* was probably the ancestor of our modern quilt. The Romans also slept on the floor on a padded pallet that they called a *culcita* and from which the modern word

"quilt" is derived. In British medieval literature and household inventories, the *culcita* had become a "cowlte" and was used both as an underlay or as a covering just as *futons* are today.

Averil Colby in her book, *Quilting*, mentions a "rich quilt wrought with coten, with crimson sendel stitched with thredes of gold,"[1] which is described in the fourteenth-century *Romance of Arthur of Lytel Brytayne*, and which she suggests may have been of Eastern origin. Ornamental "quilts" were also used in China and have been unearthed from tombs that date from as early as the Eastern Zhou dynasty (770–221 B.C.). From the archaeological descriptions it is not always easy to tell exactly how these quilts were made, but in the Eastern Zhou discovery four quilts were found in the coffin, the top one being of silk embroidered with dragons and phoenixes.[2] Although it would be misleading to exaggerate the influence of East and West upon each other in ancient times, there was a current of exchange, and from the time of the Crusades, many new and unusual textiles—embroideries, silks, woven tapestries, and perhaps quilts too—found their way to Europe from the Middle East and the Orient.

Such goods and thinking traveled along the old Silk Road, the ancient trade route that was made famous to the West by Marco Polo. It traversed the deserts and plains of Central Asia through Persia to the Mediterranean. It was near this route that the most ancient quilted piece known to man was found on the floor of a Scythian chieftain's tomb at Noin-Ula, southwest of Lake Baikal in Russia (figs. 2a and 2b). It was discovered by a Russian scientific expedition to the region from 1924 to 1926 and is now in the collection of the Leningrad branch of the Institute of Archeology of the Academy of Sciences in the U.S.S.R.

The Russians describe the piece as a "funerary carpet" and say that it was probably made some time between 100 B.C. and A.D. 200. Nomads used carpets for many different purposes. Persian carpets, for example,

1. Kimono-shaped *futon* covers were fashionable in Japan until the early twentieth century. This marvelous example was made about a hundred years ago and is a country piece; the owner probably had it dyed for her at the village dye-shop. It was customary to display one's family crest on *futon* covers—in this case a pair of facing cranes. The floral motifs are paulownia flowers and leaves. The white basting threads kept the padding from slipping. Japanese who remember sleeping under these quilts say that they were terribly heavy and nearly always damp as the filling of cotton-waste seldom dried out. Quilters are now cutting up these indigo-dyed covers to work into modern quilts. Photograph courtesy Kazuo Saito. Meiji period late nineteenth century. (Private collection)

2. The oldest known quilt in the world, it was found on the floor of a Scythian chieftain's tomb by a Russian expedition and is thought to date from between 100 B.C.–A.D. 200. The tomb was discovered at Noin-Ula near the Mongolian/Siberian border, southwest of Lake Baikal. Note the familiar spirals and the quilted cross-hatching on the borders. (Leningrad Branch of the Institute of Archaeology, Academy of Sciences of the U.S.S.R.)

were hung inside tents for warmth, to decorate the interior, to express status, and also to sleep on and use as coverings. The decorative quilted motifs on this ancient carpet—the varied patterns and lively animal appliqués—were the Scythian equivalent of the rich patterns of Persia or China, but they also link this ancient piece to a modern wholecloth quilt. We can see the familiar cross-hatching on the borders, and contour-quilting fills the bodies of the fighting animals (fig. 2c). Although the spirals in the central section of the piece appear to be couched rather than quilted, their shape can be found in many quilts today.

Following this same thread, we find a quilted slipper discarded in a rubbish dump of a fort occupied by a Tibetan garrison sometime during the eighth century A.D. on that part of the Silk Road to the north of the Taklamakan Desert near the present Sino-Russian

2a. Detail of the Siberian quilt in figure 2 showing the vigorous fighting-animal motifs in the border. The outlines appear to be couched and the bodies filled in with tightly stitched contour-quilting. A similar needlework process has also been used for the inner border. Although the beasts may be mythological, the Scythian nomadic culture was known for its marvelous "animal-style" decorative motifs that are carved or are used as felt or leather appliqués on artifacts unearthed by archaeologists. B.C. 100–A.D. 200 (Leningrad Branch of the Institute of Archaeology, Academy of Sciences of the U.S.S.R.)

3. A shoe from Mazar-tagh of quilted felt patched with leather, found on the Silk Road in the rubbish and tip of a fort occupied by a Tibetan garrison. A.D. 750–860. The pattern of overlapping curves is familiar to quilters everywhere. Length: 10″ (25.4 cm). Photograph courtesy the Trustees of the British Museum, London.

border. As you can see in figure 3, the felt upper part of the shoe was clearly cut from something else because of the way the pattern is severed at the ankle; a quilted carpet perhaps, or a quilted coat. The Tibetans still wear felt shoes, decorated nowadays with chain-stitch embroidery, their curves and shapes bearing similarities to the quilted and appliquéd patterns on the first-century chieftain's funerary carpet. The pattern of overlapping circles is familiar to quilters everywhere, but it is a pattern that is especially loved by the Japanese. They call it *seigaiha*, meaning "blue wave," and it appears etched as a pattern on the clothing of ancient pottery sculptures found in fifth-century tombs; on old and new textiles; on porcelain; as a raked pattern in a traditional Japanese garden; and nowadays, of course, on quilts.

It may be reading too much into a slipper and a nomad's carpet, but it is fascinating to conjecture that there may be a link between this north Asian quilting tradition, the kind of easily folded and stored bedding that the Japanese sleep on today—and which was also used in Rome—and the modern art of quiltmaking.

If quilting started as bedding, it soon developed, as most human inventions seem to do, to have an application in war. Quilted armor proved to be surprisingly effective against the glancing blow of an arrow, or even a sword. The Chinese, Koreans, and the Rajputs of India all wore quilted armor that may have traveled down the Silk Road to the Middle East, as some believe it was picked up from there by the Crusaders in the eleventh century and taken back to Europe. It is suspected that it was the introduction of quilted armor to Europe that led to quilted civilian

4. The Chinese have worn channel-quilted garments for centuries, and this was probably the form of stitching they used for their quilted armor. The Chinese lady in this illustration is stitching what look like military leggings. Watercolor on paper. Ca. 1790. Photograph courtesy the Trustees of the Victoria and Albert Museum, London.

5a, 5b. This beautifully quilted campaign vest belonged to one of the most colorful rulers in Japanese history, Toyotomi Hideyoshi (1537–1598), who presided over the period when myriad new ideas and influences came to Japan. Experts think that the vest was made from prequilted fabric brought as tribute from India by a British trader. The red crest on the back of the vest is a stylized paulownia flower; another version of this motif is on the *futon* cover in figure 1. Momoyama period, 1568–1598. (Kaho Educational Committee, Fukuoka Prefecture)

clothing, and perhaps subsequently to decoratively quilted bedcovers. (The hip-length quilted coat worn by the medieval foot soldier was called a "jack" and was the ancestor of our modern jacket, and also, incidentally, of the bullet-proof vest, for plates of horn or metal were inserted in the quilted channels.) Figure 4 is an eighteenth-century Chinese watercolor of a woman busily channel-stitching a pair of leggings, perhaps items of Chinese military regalia.

We find a link with quilted armor in Japan in the late 1500s. The ruler in those days was a colorful character called Hideyoshi (1537–1598), who ruled at the time described in James Clavell's book, *Shogun*, when Portuguese, Dutch, and British traders braved the dangers of the long sea voyage to investigate the fabled wealth of the "Japanns," the news of which had reached Europe through the writings of Marco Polo.

Hideyoshi was given to wearing fancy campaign vests over his armor, and because the Japanese have customarily rewarded good service with a gift of clothing or with a bolt of silk, contemporary records show that he gave the magnificently quilted vest in figures 5a and 5b to a farmer in the southern island of Kyushu who had helped him in some way during his battle to unite the country. The vest is so tightly quilted it resembles embroidery, and historians think it was probably made from a length of prequilted cloth brought from India by one of the foreign traders (probably British) as a tribute. On the back of the vest you can see the dramatic crest of a paulownia flower bestowed on Hideyoshi by the emperor.

Patchwork

Patchwork in Japan seems to have religious origins. The indigenous religion is Shinto, which endows all things, inanimate or animate, with a spirit, and this also applies to human artifacts, including textiles. Indeed, cloth commands a very special reverence and love among the Japanese. This spiritual significance came to be reinforced by ceremonial and even economic and fiscal considerations. Textiles, for example, used to be a form of currency. Woven cloth was paid as tribute to emperors and warlords, and peasants were able to avoid conscript labor by producing lengths of handwoven cloth as barter for labor. Items of clothing

or bolts of fabric were the normal way of rewarding good service as we have already seen with the quilted vest in figures 5a and 5b; and beautiful kimono, whether dyed in some simple pattern at the village dye-shop or painted by a leading artist of the day, were a woman's dearest possession and fulfilled the same role in her life as jewelry did elsewhere.

Valuable paintings were and are framed with panels of patterned silk. Treasured family heirlooms like the utensils used in the tea ceremony are always stored away in bags lovingly made of rich and rare fabrics. Buddhist sutras are rolled in fine silk wrappers. In addition to decorating their bedding, both city and country women covered their furniture with exquisitely patterned indigo-dyed wrapping cloths.

Consequently, the preservation of old fabrics has a special importance to the Japanese, and prolonging the life of old textiles is a spiritual exercise. The prolonging of life also has symbolic meaning. A patchwork robe given to a loved one or a respected superior implies the hope for a long life. The number of patches in such a garment may appropriately match the age of the recipient, especially the auspicious birthdays of seventy-seven, eighty-eight and ninety-nine. In figure 6 we illustrate a magnificent patchwork coat given by one famous Japanese general to another in 1560. The fabrics in this case are all Chinese brocades, rare and costly in those days, which would have made this coat a gift worthy of a national hero.

Figure 7 shows how this tradition of conserving old textiles continued into the nineteenth century. This beautifully worked underkimono is made of seventeenth-century scraps of printed and striped Indian cottons, which by the time this robe was made had become scarce and valuable. In 1639, fearful of foreign influence, notably Christianity, the Japanese military government had introduced a policy of national seclusion that effectively sealed Japan off from the rest of the world. Trade with other nations virtually ceased until an American naval commodore, Matthew Perry (1794–1858), forced Japan to open up again in 1853. Because of the tradition of preserving rare and beautiful fabrics, even simple cottons like those in figure 7 were carefully hoarded. The military government also forbade the merchant classes, whom they despised in spite of the fact they were the financial backbone of the country, from wearing luxury fabrics; so wealth was hidden. Forbidden fabrics were worn under drab outer garments, and the merchants and their wives even invented a special ethic to make such fashion acceptable: "hidden elegance" they called it. Therefore, the person who wore this robe was not only preserving priceless fabrics but also thumbing his nose at the authorities. This type of patchwork was known as *yosegire*, meaning "sewing together of different fragments," and we will meet it again later.

The other type of religious patchwork derives from Buddhism, which arrived in Japan thirteen hundred years ago. The Buddha lived in India in the sixth century B.C., and Buddhism gradually spread outward from India and reached Japan via Korea some time between A.D. 538 and 552. Although he was himself of princely origin, one of the precepts of the Buddha was contempt for wealth and ostentation, so he ordered his mendicant followers to renounce all worldly goods and to live by begging for food and other necessities. As an outward sign of this vow of poverty, monks had to wear patched robes. Legend says that the Buddha took the symbolic arrangement for the traditional patched robes worn by the Buddhist priesthood today from the patchwork aspect of the rice paddies in his native India.[3]

Although much of the ornamental patchwork that derives either directly or indirectly from this religious source tends to be random in construction, if you look closely at a patched Buddhist robe you will see that the patches are always arranged in an orderly sequence of panels like the vestment worn by Priest Keichu Kyuma of the Soto Zen sect in figure 8. Supposedly, this is because the scene of rice paddies that inspired the Buddha were the kind where the little fields were geometric and separated from one another by raised embankments.

In northeast Asia, priestly poverty was interpreted rather differently. These pieced robes are called *kesa* in Japan but the highest ceremonial Buddhist vestment is known as a *funzo-e*, which literally means "excreta-sweeping robe." Buddhist literature left a list of ten different sorts of rags thrown out by society from which such a robe could be made. This list includes fabric chewed by cows, gnawed by mice, charred by fire, soiled by blood from childbirth, or clothing donated by kings and court officials. Both men and women in Japan often bequeathed kimono to their

6. Seventeen different kinds of rare Chinese brocades were used to make this gorgeous patchwork coat for a famous Japanese general, Uesugi Kenshin, around 1560. Patchwork has an auspicious symbolism in the East, for by patching fabric together you prolong its life, thereby implying the hope of a long life to the recipient. Ca. 1560. (Uesugi Shrine, Yamagata Prefecture)

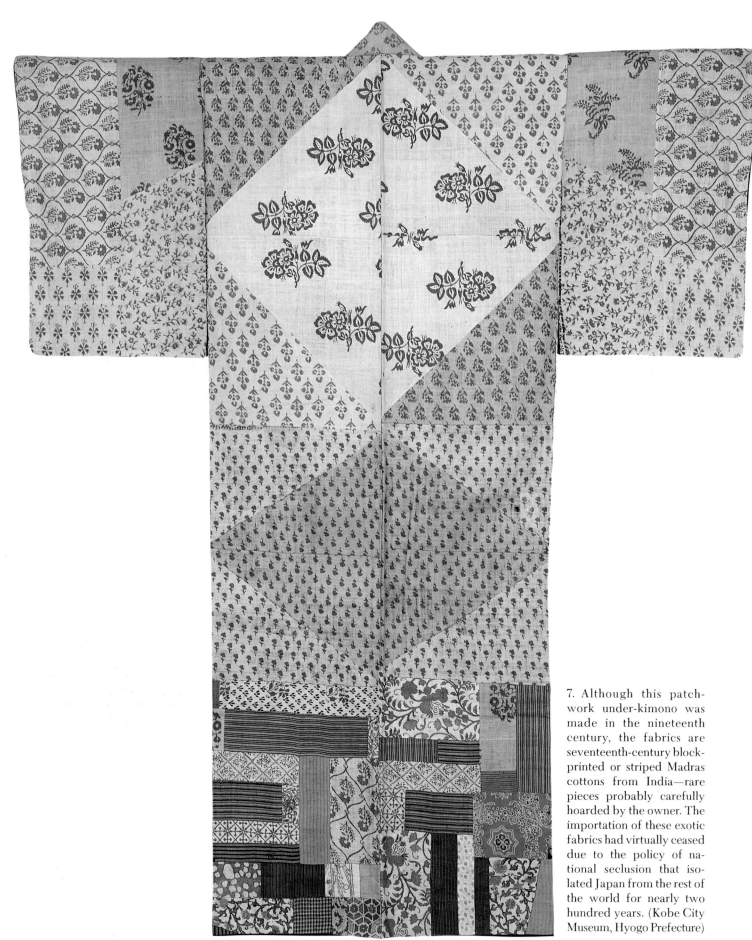

7. Although this patchwork under-kimono was made in the nineteenth century, the fabrics are seventeenth-century block-printed or striped Madras cottons from India—rare pieces probably carefully hoarded by the owner. The importation of these exotic fabrics had virtually ceased due to the policy of national seclusion that isolated Japan from the rest of the world for nearly two hundred years. (Kobe City Museum, Hyogo Prefecture)

8

local temple; textiles, as explained previously, are considered a revered form of tribute, so "excreta-sweeping robes" came to be made from patches cut from these exquisite garments.[4]

In A.D. 756, the widow of the emperor dedicated her husband's magnificent collection of art to a temple in Nara that he had built, the Todai-ji or Great Eastern Temple, which also housed a giant statue of the Buddha that he had ordered to be cast from bronze (a sixteenth-century replica can be seen there today). The collection comprised over 100,000 priceless Indian, Persian, Chinese, and Japanese textiles among many other valuable items and included several patched *funzo-e*, one of which is illustrated in figure 9. This remarkable eighth-century piece, reminiscent of some of the curved-seam work of modern American quilt artists, is actually a mixture of patchwork, appliqué, and quilting. Overlapping fragments of brown, green, and ochre silk, which have been frayed to give at least a nominal appearance of priestly poverty, are arranged on a background in the symbolic paneled order and then finely stitched down with purple thread in a form of ripple-quilting. The coloring represents the bark of a tree, but the arrangement of the silk patches gives the appearance of mountains. This particular vestment is considered to be the prototype of other similar vestments that came to be known collectively as "distant mountain" *kesa* (*kesa* being the generic name for all these patched priestly vestments).[5] The cloud-covered, mountainous scenery of their native land is never far from the minds of the Japanese. Nowadays this "distant-mountain" pattern is usually woven, and the mountain shapes are more easily discernible, as you

8. The paneled form of Buddhist patchwork can be clearly seen in the vestment worn in this photograph by Priest Keichu Kyuma of the Soto Zen sect. Photograph courtesy Keichu Kyuma and Marie Lyman of Morning Light Studio, Portland, Oregon.

9. Although this eighth-century Buddhist vestment from the Shoso-in Treasure is composed of overlapping fragments of silk, you can see that it has been arranged in the symbolic paneled order decreed by the Buddha. The pattern of this lovely, subtly toned piece represents a mountainous landscape, and it has been finely quilted with purple thread. (Shoso-in, Nara)

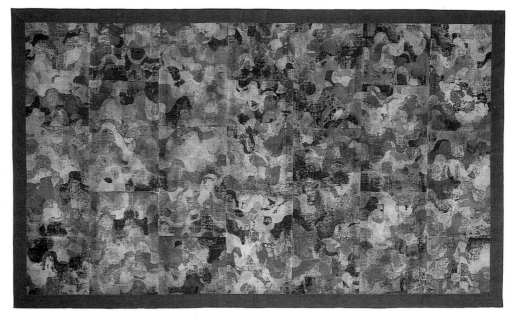

10. Sealed up in a cave temple at Dunhuang on the Silk Road for the best part of twelve hundred years, this patchwork altar valance reveals the value placed on even the tiniest scrap of silk in those days, and also gives us a priviledged glimpse of rare Tang dynasty textiles. If this were a votive offering in a desert cave, what a magnificent sight the hangings in the Buddhist temples of the Chinese capital at Chang'an (modern Xian) must have been. 20″ x 72″ (51 x 183 cm). Eighth–ninth century. Photograph courtesy the Trustees of the British Museum, London. (Stein Collection)

can see from the modern *kesa* worn by Priest Keichu Kyuma in figure 8.

Patchwork was also used to make votive offerings. Buddhism traveled from India to China and ultimately to Japan along the Silk Road, and at various points along this precarious route caravans of intrepid traders set up trading posts. Figure 10 shows a temple hanging made in the eighth century A.D. by pilgrims, perhaps, or by the people of a garrison established in the region to keep the route open. This marvelous naive piece with its triangular tabs and pennants of multicolored patched chevrons was fashioned from precious fragments of Tang dynasty silks, the most valuable gift poor people had to offer in those days.

The temple hanging was discovered in the "Cave of a Thousand Buddhas" at Dunhuang on the Chinese/Mongolian border at the western end of the Great Wall of China by Sir Auriel Stein during one of his jointly financed British/Indian expeditions in the early twentieth century. It is thought that the area was probably deserted due to the lack of water, and hundreds of priceless Buddhist artifacts were found sealed up in these caves, preserved for future generations by the extreme dryness of the region.

We also find patchwork votive offerings in Japan, both old and new. A fifteenth-century altar cloth patched from imported Chinese silks is in the collection of a temple in Kamakura near Tokyo, and figure 11 shows a section from a twentieth-century hanging made around 1930 for a temple in Shikoku. The familiar four-patch patterns, Pinwheel and Framed Square, and the ubiquitous hexagon patchwork suggest a Christian-missionary influence, but this marries happily with the Buddhist swastika of peace and the appliquéd Sanskrit characters. Patchwork cloths are offered before the altar at many Buddhist temples in Japan today.

Religious influence extends to the very needles used for fabric arts. Needles have spirits that must be laid to rest, so a memorial service known as *hari-kuyo* takes place each year at a temple in Tokyo. In figure 12 women are depositing their needles in a bed of tofu, a fine resting place for such faithful friends.

Appliqué

Appliqué was less used as a decorative medium by the Japanese than most other nations because of the early development of decorative stencil and resist-dyeing. However, its traditions may lie with the oldest inhabitants of the Japanese islands, the Ainu. This aboriginal race once inhabited all of Japan but were driven into the extreme northern island, Hokkaido, by the Japanese, a more vigorous and technically advanced people. The Ainu are a hunter/gathering race that may have its roots in north Asia, probably Siberia. They are a hirsute people without such a pronounced Oriental fold to the eye, and they used fish and animal skins for their clothing as well as cloth made from elm-bark fibers, which they chewed to make it soft enough for twining into thread.

11. This is a Japanese patchwork temple hanging that was found in the Baikoku-ji temple at Tokushima on the island of Shikoku. It was probably made during the 1930s, and the familiar American patchwork patterns suggest a Christian-missionary influence. The piecing was constructed over papers torn from account books, or old letters, including one from a Japanese soldier serving in Manchuria.

12. A memorial service for used needles and pins is held at various temples around Tokyo on February 8 each year. Women bring these faithful friends and stick them in a bed of *tofu* (beancurd) as their final resting place. The needlewomen then pray for renewed sewing skills (and no pricked fingers) during the coming year. Photograph courtesy *Mainichi Newspapers*.

13. Backview of nineteenth-century Ainu ceremonial garment showing the magnificent symmetrical appliquéd patterns embroidered with the distinctive Ainu designs. The appliqués are always cotton. This garment is made of *attush*, cloth that is woven from elm-bark fibers. Photograph courtesy the Trustees of the Victoria and Albert Museum, London.

When cotton became widely available in Japan from the middle of the eighteenth century, it came into the hands of the Ainu as a form of wages. Ainu laborers were paid in cotton cloth and they began using it to decorate their elm-bark fiber garments with wonderful symmetrical appliquéd patterns. They are great woodcarvers, and they took their patterns from this tradition and produced cloth in marvelous cabalistic designs (fig. 13). There are two forms: *nuro-oki* ("putting cloth on"), which is straightforward appliqué, and *kiri-fuse* ("cutting and spreading"), which is similar to Hawaiian appliqué. They then embroidered these with patterns based on interlocking brackets. The appliqué designs were not mere ornament, for the Ainu believed that they possessed power against evil spirits, and they attached particular importance to the decoration on the back of their garments because this protected their backs while out hunting. The more elaborate the design, of course, the more potent was its power. The Ainu survive today in small pockets in Hokkaido, and further north in Sakhalin, now under Russian control, but in Hokkaido they preserve remnants of their ancient culture for tourists (figs. 14 and 15).

The Japanese also have their own tradition of decorative stitching called *sashiko*, which is a cross between embroidery and quilting. *Sashiko* means

14. Genuine Ainu culture has all but disappeared, but they preserve elements of it for tourists. An Ainu couple stands outside a traditional thatched-straw hut. Photograph courtesy Hokkaido Tourist Board, Tokyo.

15. An important Ainu ceremony used to be the Bear Festival, when the villagers would send a bear cub they had raised back to the mountains. In this photograph Ainu women, dressed in their magnificent appliquéd clothing, are taking the cub out of a wooden cage. Photograph courtesy Hokkaido Tourist Board, Tokyo.

"little stabs," and it began originally as a running stitch to repair and strengthen the loosely woven fabrics made from the bast fibers of grasses or tree bark, which was all that the country people had for their clothing before the introduction of cotton. Women laboriously stitched several layers of cloth together to make thick, serviceable clothing for their families, and country folk would describe a winter by the number of layers needed to keep warm. "It's been a winter of three layers," they would say, or four or five. This type of tight *sashiko*-stitching was always used for firemen's clothing, and figure 16 illustrates an early twentieth-century fireman's coat that appears to have been made from several hand towels. The top one apparently was printed with the god of war and the effect seen through the tight *sashiko*-stitching is that of a tattoo. The

decorative side would have been worn inside ("hidden elegance"!), except for some festive occasion. Whoever owned this coat was a member of a private fire-brigade, for his master's name is printed on the front lapels. In the old days, merchants used to hire squads of samurai to protect their property, and during the long years of peace during Japan's self-imposed isolation from the rest of the world, fighting fires became a substitute for fighting wars.

The *sashiko* technique only became decorative when women had more leisure time, after they were released from the chore of stitching fabric together by the availability of cotton clothing. Modern *sashiko* designs are generally those that evolved in Japanese tradition or were adapted from the patterns of the figured silks used to make kimono.

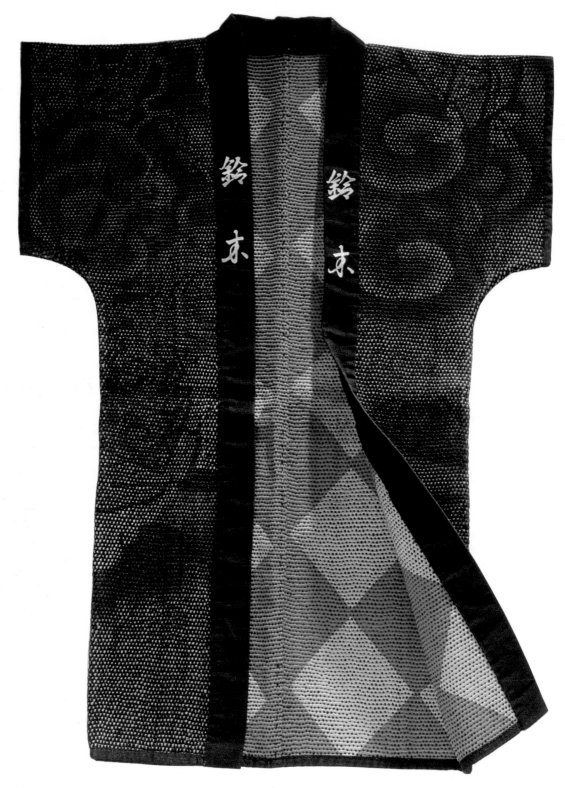

16. *Sashiko* originated as a plain running stitch that was used to repair and strengthen fabric. Women would stitch several layers of cloth together and produce a remarkably thick and durable garment like this fireman's coat. This plain form of *sashiko* was traditionally used for firemen's clothing and they would drench these garments with water before fighting the fire. Decorative *sashiko* developed during the eighteenth century when women had more leisure due to a higher level of prosperity and the widespread cultivation of cotton produced cheap, warm clothing. Early twentieth century. Photograph courtesy Kazuo Saito. (Private collection)

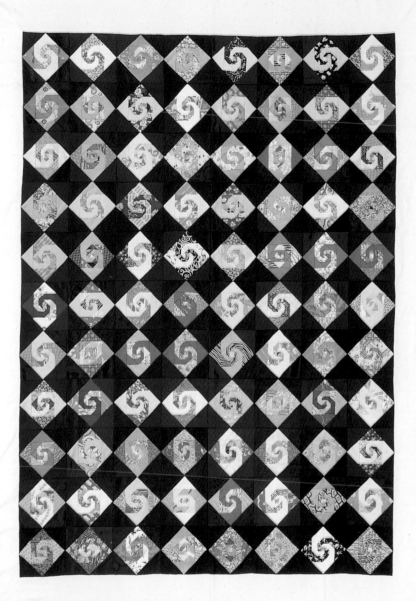

17. Iku Hara, who appears in the frontispiece to this book, used a patchwork pattern for this colorful *futon* cover that she remembers from her childhood, and she believes it to have been popular in Japan more than a hundred years ago. "In the past we used this pattern only for small items like bags or pouches," Hara says. "My mother made kimono, so I played with scraps of silk as a child, but I never visualized making a big project until I saw some American quilts in an exhibition." She made this lovely vivacious piece from scraps of silk left over from her own kimono or pieces she was given by friends. The contrast of strong color against black is reminiscent of the formal kimono worn at weddings and grand social functions.

The flash of white *sashiko*-stitching on indigo-dyed cloth is now a modern handicraft, and it is finding a new role for itself as an extra textural stitching on quilts, both in Japan and overseas.

A Final Note

Although the elements of quiltmaking were known in Japan, it is the influence of American patchwork in this country that has drawn these threads together. In the middle of the last century when the mysterious "hermit country," Japan, was opened up again to foreign trade,

Western women, who came with their husbands to live in the foreign treaty ports like Yokohama and Nagasaki, brought with them the current Victorian mania for fancy work, which included Crazy quilts and other kinds of patchwork done with silk. Iku Hara, a Japanese lady now in her eighties, who is portrayed in the frontispiece to this book with her traditional sewing box and ironing board on the floor beside her, remembers a pattern from her childhood that she still uses today to piece together beautiful *futon* covers from kimono silks (fig. 17).

Curiously, however, there was a reverse flow,

18. Before the fashion for Crazy patchwork developed in the United States, the Japanese had their own version that grew out of the traditional custom of patching pieces of fabric together, called *yosegire*. Women sewed scraps together in a random arrangement and made clothing, household items, or covered screens. In time the pattern became so popular it was stencil-dyed on cloth and on handmade paper. This is a piece of modern paper printed with a *yosegire* pattern.

unacknowledged and mostly forgotten today. Around the 1830s, *yosegire*, meaning "sewing together of different fragments," enjoyed a fashionable revival. *Yosegire* grew out of a desire to preserve and prolong the life of valuable, and particularly imported, textiles, but women now began to take pleasure in organizing patches of cloth of different colors, textures, and shapes into a pleasing design that they either used for clothing, or to make decorative cloths, or to enliven the appearance of a screen.

The patchwork undergarment made from rare Indian cottons that we saw in figure 7 was, of course, part of this trend, but it appears that *yosegire* also sometimes followed a fractured Crazy type of construction similar to the coat in figure 6. This random patterning then entered the mainstream of Japanese design and was dyed on fabric. It can be found today on porcelain, as an outline shape for decorative *sashiko* (with each "patch" filled with a different *sashiko* pattern), or printed on the lovely handmade papers that the Japanese use for their many paper crafts. Figure 18 illustrates a modern piece of handmade *washi* paper printed with a *yosegire* pattern.

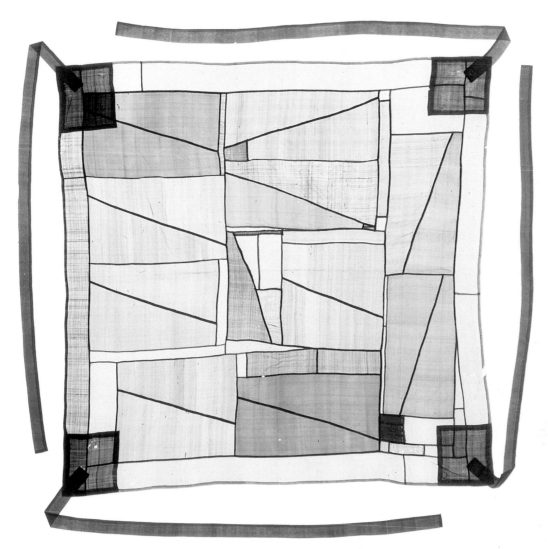

19. Korean women also shared the Japanese passion for Crazy piecing. This is a carrying cloth (*chogappo*), more ornamental than practical, made from fragments of silk gauze. It could be a modern abstract painting, yet it was made in the late nineteenth century. Photograph courtesy Japan Folkcraft Museum, Tokyo. (The Museum of Korean Embroidery, Seoul)

Yosegire patchwork was not limited to Japan, however, for Korean women also made a similar form of Crazy patchwork. Both the Koreans and the Japanese use ornamented cloths to wrap gifts for weddings, for example, or for other special occasions. In the enclosed society of nineteenth-century Korea women made patched cloths as a kind of hobby. It was believed that organizing scraps of fabric into a thing of beauty brought happiness, not only to the recipient but also to the maker. As you can see from the Korean cloth in figure 19, these women developed a refined artistic sense. This lovely piece is strikingly similar to a modern abstract painting, and there are strange echoes of Buddhist patchwork here also, for the earliest mention of these cloths was as wrappings for sutras. There were two kinds of cloths: the *pojagi*, which was nearly always embroidered and made by the ladies of the court, and the patched variety like this one, which was the work of ordinary women and called *chogappo*.

There is also a reference in a museum catalogue to "quilted" *pojagi* but no information is given to what is meant by "quilting." Given the evidence of the ripple-quilted Buddhist vestments in Japan, they were probably similarly stitched.

Soon after Japan opened up and began to participate in world affairs again, a fascination for things Japanese developed in the West. There are many famous expressions of this: Monet's paintings of waterlilies were influenced by Japanese art, Puccini composed the opera *Madame Butterfly*, and Gilbert and Sullivan wrote *The Mikado*. Fashionable women in America and Europe wore Japanese kimono as elegant gowns at

20. Six hundred and twenty-three precious scraps of Japanese silk and brocade were lovingly stitched together around 1848 to make this screen. It was given by the last shogun of Japan to a loyal supporter, Katsu Kaishu (1823–1899), as an honored gift. It may have been a similar screen that was exhibited at the Centennial Exposition in Philadelphia in 1876 and started the vogue for Crazy patchwork. A great-grandson of Katsu Kaishu has donated the screen to a museum due to open in Tokyo in 1992–1993. Photograph courtesy Yoshimasa Katsu.

soirées, which has been captured by the American painter James Abbot McNeill Whistler (1834–1903) in his lovely painting *Caprice in Purple and Gold No. 2: The Golden Screen*. In patchwork, the Crazy quilt became the rage, and this style was also known as "Japanese patchwork."

The American public's imagination was captured by Japan after Japanese decorative arts were displayed for the first time in the United States at the Philadelphia Centennial Exposition in 1876. In her book *Crazy Quilts*, Penny McMorris explains that it may have been a screen, or a group of screens, exhibited in the Japanese pavillion that "provided the design influence that came to maturity in the crazy quilt. Some of the screens exhibited there were described as being covered with textured gilt paper ornamented with patches of various materials that had painted, embroidered, or quilted designs."[6]

This screen (or screens) may have been covered with the kind of paper shown in figure 18, or it may actually

20a. Here you can see the silk and brocade pieces in greater detail. They are all woven fabrics and were probably used for scroll-mountings or furnishings like armrests or floor cushions. The majority of the fabrics date from the early nineteenth century, but there are a few priceless fragments from the late 1400s. Many woven Japanese fabrics look as if they are over-embroidered—a complex weaving technique

acquired from China. If a screen similar to this example was exhibited at Philadelphia in 1876, it is quite possible that the Victorian ladies believed that these exquisite silk patches were embroidered and therefore copied the idea for their Crazy quilts. At the start of the fad, Crazy patchwork was known as "Japanese patchwork." Photograph courtesy Yoshimasa Katsu.

have been covered with patches of fabric in the *yosegire* style illustrated in figures 20 and 20a. There is mystery and romance attached to this particular screen. It contains 623 separate fragments of beautiful Japanese silks and brocades. Some of the pieces are of the late fifteenth century, but most are from the Bunsei era (1818–1830), and it is thought that the screen was probably made around 1848. The screen must have been highly valued as it belonged to the family of the last Japanese shogun. The feudal-style shogunate was abolished in 1868 after 250 years of isolationist rule by a team of vigorous new leaders who reestablished imperial rule under the young emperor Meiji, whose reign-name defines the era. The deposed shogun gave this screen to a loyal supporter, Katsu Kaishu (1823–1899), a distinguished statesman who succeeded, for a time, in straddling the transition between regimes and

who is known today as the founder of the Japanese navy.

The screen remained in the possession of the Katsu family until quite recently, and although we shall probably never know by whom it was made or how it came to be one of the shogun's treasures, it seems possible that if such a screen was sufficiently admired by the ruling classes to be given as an honored reward for loyal service, then a similar screen could well have been included in the display of Japanese decorative arts at the Centennial Exposition in Philadelphia in 1876, and as Penny McMorris explains, started the vogue for Crazy quilts. The Katsu family does not believe that this particular screen ever left Japan, but they do say that it was one of two, and possibly three, such screens in existence at that time.

We are extremely fortunate to be able to show

photographs of it. Yoshimasa Katsu, a great-grandson of the statesman, donated it to a museum foundation in Tokyo some years ago, but until the proposed museum opens, probably in 1992–1993, the screen remains locked away in a storeroom and inaccessible both to the public and its previous owners. Another descendant of Katsu Kaishu, his great-granddaughter Mrs. Sumiko Gomi, approached her second cousin Yoshimasa Katsu on our behalf, and he was kind enough to lend us some family snapshots, and these are the illustrations in figures 20 and 20a. Professional photographs will have to be made when the new owners are prepared to exhibit this fascinating work.

Romance also has a place in this story, an American romance at that. William Whitney, a director of a business college in Newark, New Jersey, and a descendant of the inventor Eli Whitney, was invited by the new Meiji government to establish a similar business school in Tokyo. He arrived in Japan in 1875 accompanied by his wife, son, and two daughters—the elder, Clara, was then fourteen—only to find that government support for the scheme had evaporated. The family, who had spent all their money to pay for the voyage to Japan, faced penury. However, private backing was provided by Katsu Kaishu, who lent money and a house to the Whitneys and encouraged William to start up on his own. Being people of grit and strong religious convictions, the Whitneys stayed on and made a success of the project.

Clara's initial distaste for the "heathen people" turned to tenderness, and she ended up marrying Kaji Umetaro, one of Katsu Kaishu's sons by a concubine, and they had six children. She was a lively, witty girl, who kept a diary describing the early years when Japan was emerging from its feudal state into the modern age. The diary was edited and published under the title *Clara's Diary, an American Girl in Meiji Japan*.[7] In the entry for May 10, 1876, Clara records a dinner that the Whitneys gave for a princely family of the deposed shogun's clan. "After dinner, which most of them seemed to enjoy, Mama entertained the ladies by exhibiting examples of her household skill, the sewing machine, dresses, quilts, comforters, etc., which interested them more than anything."[8]

The diary also reveals that in the days of poverty Clara taught sewing to a group of Japanese ladies. As her mother was obviously a quiltmaker, one longs to know whether she included ornamental patchwork in her classes, and if so, was there a cultural exchange: *yosegire* versus American block patchwork? Who knows; it is possible that Clara may even have been inspired by this screen. She was a frequent visitor to the Katsu household, where it would probably have been proudly displayed.

The trading exchange between East and West that grew up all those centuries ago along the old Silk Road was therefore still actively at work, and our hope is that it will continue vigorously, aided a little by our book. In the chapters that follow, you will see what surprising and delightful results the Japanese are achieving in their patchwork today. The historical threads of their patchwork tradition are all present here: the love of fabric, the careful reworking of valuable and treasured fragments, the desire to preserve and restore textiles that have seen better days, and also the spiritual associations of giving. Many of these quilts made on the other side of the world are dedicated to the spirit of a relative. Come, step "through the looking glass" and enjoy these fascinating and beautiful works with us.

JILL LIDDELL

20

American Patterns — Hybrid Quilts

We have called the quilts in this section "hybrid" because they are the offspring of two different species, American and Japanese. Hybrids are noted for their energy and this quality is immediately apparent in these well-made "American-quilts-with-a difference."

The differences are sometimes slight, sometimes eye-catching, and in some cases the American characteristics are hardly apparent. During the absorption of American patchwork by Japanese culture, the American patterns and settings remain dominant, and only the detail and execution show Japanese characteristics (figs. 1, 2). But as the absorption process advances, the "Japaneseness" increases until, as you will see in the next section, the

21. *Airing the Quilts* by Megumi Komoda, Tokyo. 1985. 67″ x 67″ (170 x 170 cm). Solid and printed cottons. Hand-pieced, appliquéd, and quilted. An American quilt in style, coloring, and format, and a joyful expression of this quiltmaker's curiosity about country life in the United States, where she lived for a while and learned her quiltmaking. A quilt, perhaps, that illustrates the strong tie the Japanese have with America and American culture. "All my quilts are visible records of my memories," Komoda tells us. "I made this one for my group's exhibition after I returned to Tokyo, and it commemorates a quilt auction I went to at a farm outside Philadelphia." Komoda always makes her quilts by hand ("I find machine-made quilts look stiff"), but she is known as "Pinky" Komoda by Japanese editors because of her bright American coloring—she always includes pink somewhere in her quilts. This enchanting piece with its clever use of myriad prints was reproduced on the cover of *Patchwork Quilt Tsūshin*, No. 11, and in the February 1987 edition of *Quilter's Newsletter Magazine* in the U.S.

22. *Hibiscus* by Yoshiko Itaya, Yokohama. 1984. 80″ x 66″ (203 x 168 cm). Broadcloth and sheeting. Hand-appliquéd and quilted. Itaya tells us that she had always worked with antique colors before—browns and rusts—and she wanted to try her hand at using pure color, but she got bored while appliquéing the red hibiscus flowers, so she decided to break the monotony by including some ravishing hummingbirds to draw the eye away from the regularity of the design. These little birds add an unusual piquancy to this beautiful appliqué in the Hawaiian style. Note the birds at the lower right and left emerging from the edge of the quilt. Yoshiko says of her quiltmaking, "every stitch is for my family." One of her quilts won Best of Show at a nationwide contest organized by a firm of fabric manufacturers.

design, style, and color harmonies become truly Japanese.

In this section we find the classic Log Cabin pattern interpreted in original ways; the colors of late fall in America and Japan celebrated in a cascade of glowing reds that the quiltmaker tells us she hopes will also suggest "folds of cloth" (the abiding love the Japanese have for textiles will become readily apparent as you read the captions in this book); American stained-glass techniques illustrate Japanese symbolism in a cloisonné setting; and the traditional Medallion quilt has been reinterpreted with Japanese calligraphy at its core. See for yourself how interestingly the Japanese handle other American styles and patterns, and the vigor shines through. These are hybrid plants of high quality, fit to flourish in any "garden," East or West.

Most of the quilts are handmade, not because the Japanese don't have sewing machines—nearly all households have a sophisticated machine for doing household repairs, but because the Japanese like "doing it for real." "If that is the way it should be done, then that is the way it will be done": an attitude that comes from their long and honorable tradition of handmade crafts. But hybrid energy enters into the very execution of these quilts; nor are Japanese quiltmakers unproductive. Many produce several quilts a year, and big ones too, all lovingly hand-stitched, including putting the blocks together and sewing on the borders. They enjoy working with their hands and it shows.

The Japanese continue to enjoy American patterns and settings, and, although a more endemic style is developing, hybrid quilts remain an important part of the quilting vocabulary of Japan. You will find stunning examples in the other sections further on.

23. *Denshoh* ("A Legend") by Emiko Toda Loeb, New York City. 1986. 75″ x 58″ (192 x 147 cm). Antique Japanese *aizome* and colored stencil-dyed cottons. Machine-pieced. The varied textures and the sensational woven effect this quiltmaker has achieved by the clever manipulation of color and fabric make this a unique Log Cabin quilt. It is a real hybrid, for although the pattern is an American classic, the coloring and fabrics are traditionally Japanese. "I visualized working with our lovely old fabrics after I had studied American antique quilts because I felt Japanese textiles would help me express my inner self in a tangible form," Loeb explains. "People tell me my quilts look Japanese, but I don't set out deliberately to make them look that way." She believes patchwork is an international medium, but here we find strong Japanese associations in the traditional blue-and-white color scheme and the rich effect created by the juxtaposition of the stenciled prints. This is a remarkable quilt that required expert design skills and dexterity, for Loeb pieced her Log Cabin pattern so that it was double-sided. As she sewed each indigo-blue "log," she sewed a red "log" on at the back at the same time, thus making it completely reversible—a quilt for all seasons. Photograph courtesy the artist.

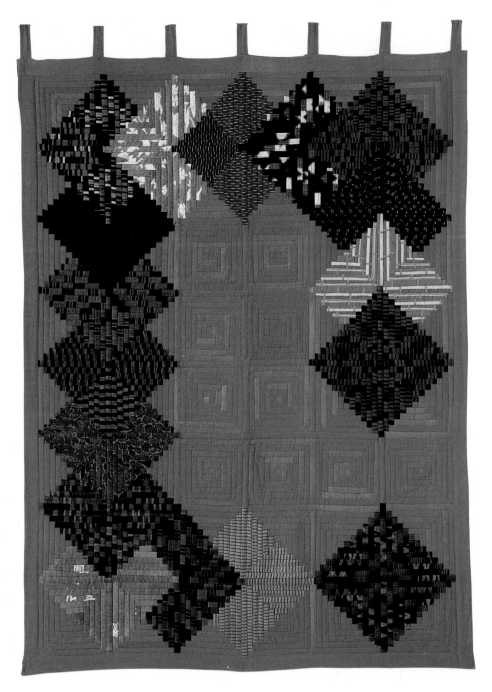

23a. The Japanese influence is also evident on the reverse side of *Denshoh*. A red background is traditionally celebratory, and we can also see a well-known Japanese artistic convention in the way Loeb has positioned her colored Log Cabin blocks so that they overlap and seemingly "float" on the surface. The Japanese passion for asymmetry is illustrated by the omission of a block on the lower right side. Symmetry and balanced designs disturb the Japanese, and they will usually find a way of introducing some element of irregularity. Emiko Toda Loeb now lives in New York City where she teaches and runs the large "New Winds Group." Two quilts made by one of her students also appear in this section. Her work has been widely exhibited in the U.S.A. and Japan, and it has also been featured in *Patchwork Quilt Tsūshin*, *Quilter's Newsletter Magazine*, and the 1988 edition of *The Quilt Engagement Calendar*. Photograph courtesy the artist.

24. *Elements* by Akio Kawamoto, Tokyo. 1982. 86″ x 71″ (218 x 180 cm). Hand-dyed "Stained Glass" cottons. Machined-pieced. This strangely beautiful Log Cabin quilt with its varied coloring and shifting fractured blocks was made by a very unusual Japanese, a man who was one of the earliest pioneers of American quiltmaking in Japan. Akio Kawamoto worked mostly as a costume designer for the stage, but opened a shop in Tokyo in the early seventies, where he sold antique American quilts and quilting supplies. He started making quilts himself at his wife's suggestion, and this hybrid was a sort of catharsis. "It represents my state of mind at the time," he tells us. "I was depressed and angry, so I deliberately distorted the pattern—changing the shapes and colors of each block, working some as triangles, some as circles, others as random strips, and I finished it in fifty-three hours working nonstop." The refracted coloring redolent of stained glass comes from his special hand-dyed fabric. He studied stained-glass-making in the United States, but injured his hand. Because he wanted to continue experimenting with optical effects when he returned to Tokyo, he dyed fabric and worked with that instead. He made a number of these arbitrary Log Cabins but has now moved on to new endeavors. One of his most recent quilts is illustrated in figure 41.

25. *Crazy Medallion* by Michiyo Tanaka, Kyoto. 1980. 59″ x 59″ (150 x 150 cm). Cotton prints and solids; sarasa (a type of printed batik); ramie (a fine kimono fabric made from plant fibers). Hand-pieced, Crazy patchwork, hand-quilted. This engaging medallion with its unusual combination of geometric piecing framed by Crazy borders is an illustration of the way many Japanese quiltmakers in the early days tried to counteract traditional American symmetry with randomness. The Japanese feel uncomfortable with symmetry, preferring the vitality and movement of the irregular and the oblique, a feature of their design that will become apparent in other sections of this book. Tanaka was given a piece of old Japanese batik by a friend and decided to use it to frame a classic American Feathered Star ("I wanted to try and capture the smell of the sun of old America"), but because she feels happier using fabric freely, she combined this symmetrical pattern with her favorite Crazy patchwork. Her quilting is also unorthodox. The white area that frames the central star is meticulously quilted in the feather design, but when it came to the Crazy borders, Tanaka went to town and quilted them with whatever designs took her fancy. This delightful work appeared first in *Patchwork Quilt Tsūshin*, where it caught the eye of the editor of *Quilter's Newsletter Magazine*, and it was then featured on the cover of the June 1985 issue.

26. *Decoy* by Mikiko Misawa, Kumamoto City, Kumamoto Prefecture. 1984. 79″ x 79″ (200 x 200 cm). Cotton dress fabrics, cotton velvets. Hand-pieced, appliquéd, and quilted. It was the story of "The Ugly Duckling" by Hans Christian Andersen that inspired this wonderfully colorful kaleidoscopic quilt. The scene is where the ugly duckling mistakes a decoy in the middle of the lake for its mother. Although Western in both design and fabric, Misawa has fashioned numerous little minipatchwork blocks such as a Nine Patch, Variable Star, Schoolhouse, or Bow Tie, which she has cunningly concealed in the hand string-pieced blocks ("they represent the duckling's adventures"). The Japanese enjoy disguising beauty in unexpected places. When government regulations in the eighteenth century made it an offense to wear colorful clothing, men and women hid luxurious—and forbidden—fabrics under drab outer clothing. This lovely quilt appeared on the cover of *Patchwork Quilt Tsūshin*, No. 12, while another quilt of hers won an award on her prefectural craft exhibition. "I never get tired of patchwork," Misawa says, "and I hope by stitching away I am setting an example to my children. Handwork makes people gentle, and those around them gentle too."

27. *Song of the Fans* by Ritsuko Shino, Ryugasaki City, Ibaragi Prefecture. 1983. 41″ x 35″ (103 x 89 cm). Cotton prints, cotton velvet, and indigo-dyed cottons. Hand-pieced and hand-quilted. As a child, the maker of this richly colored fan quilt used to gaze longingly at the beautiful hand-painted and embroidered kimono and obi that her mother made and kept folded away in a chest. The memory lingered, so when Ritsuko Shino moved from Tokyo to the country, she decided to translate these childhood memories into a quilt. She found the border fabric first and chose the pieced fan pattern to complement it, but it is the randomly scattered fans on the border that gives this quilt its uniquely Japanese look. Although she worked with cotton fabrics, she tried to re-create the feel of old Japanese silk by a careful choice of color. "I don't make detailed plans first," Shino tells us, "because I like to let my creativity flow." This spontaneous process led her to introduce a diagonal line of contrasting blue fans, a somewhat irrational choice to a Western eye, but which emphasizes the glow of the rest of the quilt. The exquisitely quilted border patterns echo the water ripples seen on some of the printed fans.

28. *Ocean* by Junko Okuyama, Fort Lee, New Jersey. 1986. 79″ x 79″ (200 x 200 cm). Cotton, polycottons, cotton/wool blends, and woolens. Hand-pieced. Machine-assembled. Hand-quilted. As a schoolgirl in Japan the maker of this wonderfully lively work made some small patchwork projects, but after moving to the United States, she was so stimulated by the beauty of antique American quilts that she joined Emiko Toda Loeb's "New Winds Group" and took up quiltmaking seriously. This idiosyncratic interpretation of the classic Ocean Waves pattern is her third quilt (hence the number "three" embroidered in the bottom right corner). It was made for the "New Winds Group" exhibition in Manhattan in 1986. "I didn't decide on the coloring before I began," Okuyama tells us, "and I pieced each block individually, but I found the process of setting them together was the most enjoyable part." She says that she is influenced by Amish coloring, and the vivid blue of her "ocean" is reminiscent of the Indiana Amish palette. An "Amish" attitude to design is also demonstrated by the way some of her blocks bleed into one another—the sort of spontaneous effect that would delight a Japanese artist too. She has added a Japanese touch by quilting fans in the alternate squares. *Ocean* was illustrated in the 1988 edition of *The Quilt Engagement Calendar*. Photograph courtesy the artist.

29. *Late Fall* by Junko Okuyama, Fort Lee, New Jersey. 1987. 75″ x 78″ (190 x 198 cm). Cottons, wool, polyester, and rayon. Mostly hand-pieced, hand-quilted. In this radiantly colored work, Junko Okuyama has once again demonstrated her wonderful sense of color. The symbolism here is the fall coloring of both her native Japan and the United States. "I wanted to use straight lines in a way that one would perceive as curved," she explains. "So I did it by having a large number of small blocks with minute changes of proportion in the angles of the triangles, and I tried to work the coloring to suggest folds of cloth." She bought most of her fabric in the U.S., but the quilt contains one or two traditional Japanese prints. "I thoroughly enjoyed the designing and the piecing," she says "but the repetitive quilting pattern made it hard to keep going!" Because this quilt is her fourth, she has embroidered "four" at the bottom right, a nice way of recording the sequence of one's work. *Late Fall* is illustrated in the 1989 edition of *The Quilt Engagement Calendar*. Photograph courtesy the artist.

30. *Toy Windmill* by Ai Mitsuhashi, Ishikari Gun, Hokkaido. 1982. 66″ x 85″ (168 x 216 cm). Cotton sateens and cotton sheeting. Hand-pieced and quilted. *Futons* are covered with brightly colored and beautifully patterned fabrics in Japan which, in spite of the fact they are then hidden from view by a sheet or a zipped cover, the Japanese know, and enjoy knowing, that they are there. Mitsuhashi bought samples of these sateens to make this lovely quilt redolent of colorful toy windmills whirling away against a night sky, celebrating some festival perhaps. "My children take an interest in my quilts," she explains "and often suggest designs." In order to introduce a Japanese flavor to her classic American design, Mitsuhashi quilted the alternative blocks with a pattern derived from a heraldic crest (*kamon*). The inner quilted border is also Japanese, a pattern known as *higaki*, meaning "braided fence," a type of country fencing made from woven strips of wood. In keeping with her cross-cultural plan, Mitsuhashi finished the quilt with a border of the traditional Flying Geese pattern. "Quiltmaking means consolation and friendship to me," she tells us. "When I first moved from Tokyo to Hokkaido, I had no friends, but my quilts made friends for me." She held a solo show in Hokkaido in May 1986.

31. *Stained-Glass Sampler* by Yukiko Saito, Bloomfield Hills, Michigan. 1981. 83″ x 55″ (210 x 140 cm). Old *furoshiki* (this is a square cloth that the Japanese use as a carryall). Kimono cottons and hand-dyed sheeting. Stained-glass appliqué and hand-quilted. Saito made this ravishingly colored example of a popular American appliqué technique truly Japanese by her choice of subject matter. The motifs represent the passing of the seasons: bamboo for winter, cherry blossoms for spring, and fans for summer. She has also commemorated two annual children's festivals: Girls' Festival on March 3 (the two little dolls at the bottom left of the center medallion) and Boys' Day (now sometimes called Children's Festival) on May 5 (the samurai helmet below). "I had previously worked only with blue-and-white fabrics, so this was my first adventure with color," she tells us. Saito was taught to sew by her mother, and before she went to live in the United States she ran a group in her hometown. "Now I have switched from making quilts to studying American crafts, such as Pennsylvania Dutch design. There will be time for quilts later, but in the meantime, America offers too many exciting challenges." This beautifully worked piece appeared on the cover of *Patchwork Quilt Tsūshin*, No. 8, and another of her quilts was featured in *Hands All Around*.

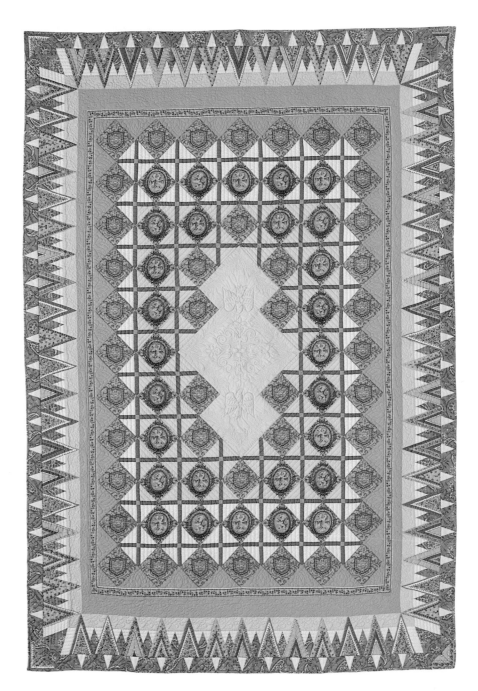

32. *Eagle and Crest Medallion* by Kayoko Konishi, Sendai City, Miyagi Prefecture. 1979. 89″ x 49″ (225 x 125 cm). Antique sarasa (a type of printed batik). Hand-pieced with trapunto work in the center, hand-quilted. The unusual coloring of this Medallion quilt is reflected in the fabrics that were given to Konishi by her grandmother. Although this type of print is Japanese, its antecedents came originally from India, having been brought to Japan in the sixteenth century by the Dutch, British, or the Portuguese, who conducted a trilateral trade in those days between India, Indonesia, and Japan: cottons from India, spices from Java, and porcelain from Japan, which were then taken back and sold in Europe. (Similar Indian prints were the forerunners of the Scottish paisleys and the Provençal cottons of France.) Fifty or sixty years ago, when the particular sarasa fabric used here by Konishi was printed, European-style motifs were fashionable, so she decided to make the European "crests" the main focus of her design. The quilting pattern in the center medallion is derived from these heraldic crests, while her ingenious double border effectively shows off the "Indian" origins of this now thoroughly assimilated Japanese fabric. Konishi taught herself how to do patchwork after seeing American quilts in a home-decorating magazine in the seventies. She now runs a quilt shop and organizes a group of her own.

33. *Cosmos Flowers* by Sumiko Maeda, Kumamoto City, Kumamoto Prefecture. 1985. 46″ x 35″ (116 x 89 cm). Hand-dyed cotton lawns. Hand-pieced and quilted. The sight of wild cosmos (a type of aster) growing on a hillside with their petals touching and overlapping, and glowing in the evening light, was the inspiration for this subtly colored quilt. Maeda wanted to make a contemporary quilt rather than try and reproduce the scene in appliqué, so she devised a design that is based on a pattern well known to both Americans and Japanese. Americans call the pattern Orange Peel, while in Japan it has ancient courtly origins and is called Seven Treasures. This lovely piece, then, is perhaps less of a hybrid than an example of the universality of design. Maeda hand-dyed white lawn in different shades of pink and lavender in order to achieve the range of tones she wanted. She is the leader of a large quilt group, and one of their group efforts is illustrated in figure 38. She taught herself patchwork and one of her quilts won Grand Prix in a nationwide needlework contest. She tells us eloquently that her quilts are "the footsteps of my life."

34. *The Promise of Spring* by Rieko Hattori, Kawasaki City, Kanagawa Prefecture. 1982. 22″ x 22″ (55 x 55 cm). Silks and cottons. Hand-pieced, appliquéd, and quilted. It was only after seeing photographs of the 1976 Holstein exhibition that Rieko Hattori realized how she could put her collection of Japanese fabrics to good use, although it was some years before she could actually bring herself to work with these precious silks. This exquisite piece is a perfect illustration of the Japanese art of miniaturization (it is only 22″ square) set in a traditional American Medallion format. Hattori feels she is best at realistic designs, so she either used fabric that had been stencil-dyed with auspicious motifs or made appliquéd blocks of popular children's toys associated with the New Year celebrations, when children anticipate the coming of spring. Among the blocks you will find plum blossom, bamboo fronds, and in the top center block stylized shapes that represent pine boughs—a traditional floral combination that symbolizes good luck. Hattori says she regards quiltmaking as a way of creating an identity for herself. Two other miniature quilts by Hattori are illustrated in figures 69 and 71.

35. *The Dream of the Braves* by Michiko Kuratani, Nagano City, Nagano Prefecture. 1985. 76″ x 61″ (194 x 156 cm). Old neckties and old kimono fabrics. Hand-pieced, appliquéd, and quilted. After her husband died, Kuratani took up quiltmaking "to keep my brain going and my memory alive," and says she has found a second life for herself. "Quiltmaking encouraged me to take up painting and graphic design, and I have learned so much about color." She made this richly hued quilt from old neckties belonging to her late husband and son, and the title is taken from a famous Japanese poem about a samurai that Kuratani likens to a modern businessman. "His life is still a battleground," she says. The top part of the quilt represents youth, and the rest signifies "the passing of time." She added little appliqués to lighten it: balloons and a rainbow for the joys of childhood; a symbolic umbrella under which to find shelter during "the rains of life"; and a pine tree for the stability of old age. Kuratani is sixty years old, and she writes poetry that she polishes in her mind as she quilts. Her work has been exhibited, and she has used her quilts to illustrate a book she published of her husband's essays. "I stitch what time is left to me in my quilts," she tells us, "and I relive my youth through color." Here is a heartwarming example of how American quiltmaking transformed the life of a Japanese who had the courage to tackle this rewarding craft late in life.

36. *Medallion Sampler* by Shoko Ishio, Hakodate City, Hokkaido. 1984. 90″ x 72″ (229 x 183 cm). Cottons and silks. Hand-pieced and hand-quilted. This beautifully worked quilt with its myriad American patchwork patterns may look Western, but two features identify its Japanese origins: the idiosyncratic placement of a half block in the lower right corner and the two maverick patches of color in the top and bottom borders. As we saw in Emiko Toda Loeb's quilt in figure 23a, the Japanese dislike the monotony of symmetrical design and will nearly always contrive to break symmetry in some way, even if it is barely discernible to outsiders. Ishio tells us that she traded fabric with her friends and has used both cotton and silks to fashion her miniblocks. The exquisitely quilted "square-within-a-square" design on the inner medallion and the outer borders is based on a pattern derived from a nest of measuring boxes used for the standard measurement of grains and liquids. It is a pattern you find often in Japan, and it was adopted as a family crest by a well-known line of *kabuki* actors who still use it today. This is Ishio's fifth quilt, but she says she is still hoping to make the "quilt of her dreams."

37. *High School Memory* by Misako Makino, Tokorozawa City, Saitama Prefecture. 1987. 73″ x 69″ (185 x 175 cm). Cottons. Hand-pieced, appliquéd, embroidered, and quilted. The Japanese have taken readily to friendship and commemorative quilts, and Misako Makino made this unusual piece to commemorate the 1982 Inter-High School Softball Championships in which her daughter participated. "My husband suggested the design," she tells us. "Each block is made from a different colored print or solid and is embroidered with the name of one of my daughter's teammates or the autograph of the team coaches. I went to many of the matches, so I got to know everybody really well. You will find a picture of the school and the logos of some of the schools my daughter's team played. The telephone number is that of a private home where she stayed for an away-from-home match. It's a real commemorative quilt!" Makino teaches deaf children and says she is glad to have a hobby that is so different from her rather exacting profession. "As well as relaxing me, quilting also keeps me young!" Makino's work has won her awards in two regional craft exhibitions. She is a self-taught quiltmaker.

38. *The Coaster Quilt*. A group quilt made by "The Fabric and Thread Quilters" organized by Sumiko Maeda, Kumamoto City, Kumamoto Prefecture. 1983. 47″ x 87″ (120 x 220 cm). Cotton broadcloth, cotton prints, and Japanese sheeting. Hand-pieced. Maeda runs a large quilt group ("It began as a small class but kept on growing"), and every time the group puts on an exhibition she likes the members to enter a group quilt. She actually used this one as a teaching process for her students. The basic colors were mutually agreed upon, and in order to choose the patterns, the members played an eliminating game similar to our "Scissors, Stone, Paper" that you see children playing all over Japan. The victor then chose her favorite pattern, and of the 220 represented no two are alike. "I thought it would be more unusual if the individual blocks were round, like coasters," Maeda says, "so they were all backed and quilted individually and then joined together later." One of Maeda's own quilts is illustrated in figure 33.

39. *Dream Quilt* by Yoshie Shimizu, Takatsuki City, Osaka. 1985. 89″ x 72″ (226 x 182 cm). Indigo cottons, stripes, stencil-dyed fabrics, and vegetable-dyed cottons. Hand-pieced, appliquéd, reverse-appliquéd, and quilted. The inspiration behind this magnificently worked quilt is truly cross-cultural. The symmetrical medallion is Western, but the calligraphy in the center immediately identifies its Japanese origin. Shimizu explains that she was influenced by the work of the famous Japanese dye artist Keisuke Serizawa, who incorporated calligraphy in much of his work, "but I interpreted his idea in my own way." The central character means "dream," and it was written for her in an elegant form by her calligraphy teacher. The characters in the four corner blocks are taken from an ancient book of Japanese seals. ("We use a seal for official confirmation like a Westerner uses a signature.") The two on the left are her name and the two on the right are variations of the character for the word "dream." The artist worked these in reverse-appliqué and has also included four finely appliquéd knots that may appear to owe something to Celtic interlace art, but knots also have a mystical association in Japan. Elaborately intertwined gold and silver "treasure knots" are used to decorate gifts with a different type of knot used for different occasions.

40. *Winter at Hewton* by Helen Tynan, Devonshire, England. 1983. 48″ x 96″ (122 x 244 cm). Cotton, silks, synthetics, satin. Hand-appliquéd and quilted. This is the work of a British quiltmaker influenced by Japanese art and who has borrowed the Japanese medium of a four-paneled screen to create a richly textured illustration of the Devonshire countryside near her home. Trained as a fine artist at the University of London, Tynan says she is fascinated by the problems of creating images of people, architecture, and landscape through the medium of appliqué and piecework. "It combines my training as a painter, my love of fabrics, and my interest in the visual world around me in a totally absorbing way," she tells us. "And because quiltmaking is a flat medium, it is essential when drawing and cutting figures, buildings, or natural forms to simplify and refine them. Japanese art epitomizes an expressiveness through simplicity that has appealed to artists and designers from the late nineteenth century onward. This I try to achieve through the subject matter of my own time and place." Tynan taught art in London for a number of years but became a full-time professional quiltmaker in 1980. Her visually stunning work has been widely exhibited in Britain, Berlin, and Dubai, and her quilts have also appeared in various U.K. publications. Photograph courtesy the artist.

41. *Untitled*. This is one of a series of quilts using curved-pieced geometric designs by Akio Kawamoto, Tokyo. 1985. 51″ x 51″ (130 x 130 cm). Hand-dyed cotton. Hand-pieced, partially appliquéd, hand-quilted. Kawamoto is one of Japan's leading quiltmakers and possibly its only male quiltmaker. He began his career by making Log Cabin quilts but has now moved on to experimenting with curved shapes and piecing. This strong, assertive quilt with its lovely opalescent coloring is very different from his other unschematic work seen earlier (fig. 24). In order to do this complex curved work successfully, Kawamoto has evolved a new way of piecing that owes something to the old English patchwork method using backing paper. Kawamoto has now exchanged the quilt shop he once owned for a gift shop where he sells the lovely "stained-glass fabrics" that he dyes to simulate the refracted light of true stained glass. "I am constantly seeing new effects," he says. "Sometimes the fabrics look like suede or leather and at other times they gleam like silk." Kawamoto teaches professionally, and his impressive quilts line the walls of his shop.

41a. Kawamoto uses a cardboard template to cut his fabric and then snips the curved edge. Photographs courtesy Shoshi Ayabe.

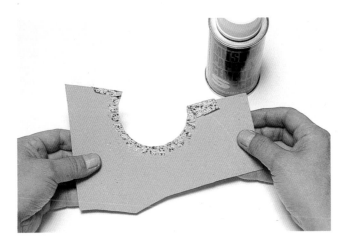

41b. He pastes the curved edge over the template.

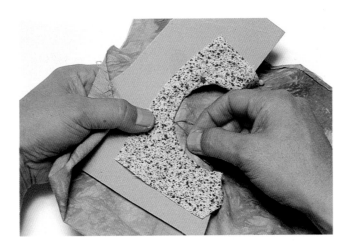

41c. And top stitches it to the adjoining fabric.

41d. Then he pulls the stitched piece off the card.

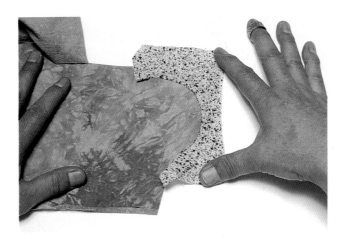

41e. After pressing, the curved section lies completely flat.

42. *Banquet Under the Trees* by Isako Murakami, Sayama City, Saitama Prefecture. 1984. 65″ x 61″ (164 x 156 cm). Kimono fabrics. Hand-pieced, appliquéd, and quilted. This intricately pieced quilt with its soft mellow coloring commemorates a wedding. Murakami was given a silk wedding kimono, obi, and traditional silk wedding underwear by a friend and has used all of it in her quilt including the kimono lining ("I used that for the backing, and the binding was made from the obi.") The silk for wedding kimono is very thick, and Murakami tells us that because she knew it would be impossible to quilt, she devised the unusual pattern based on a Log Cabin construction to get over this hurdle. "I pieced the 'logs' by hand into triangles first (you can see these in the corner blocks), and then sewed them together to form hexagons." She says she wanted to create the idea of a banquet held out of doors under the trees, so the pieced area in the center reflects the changing tints of autumn, while the appliquéd motifs in the top and bottom borders (the scrumptious cake and the lacquer box containing sushi) elaborate her pastoral theme of a *déjeuner sur l'herbe*.

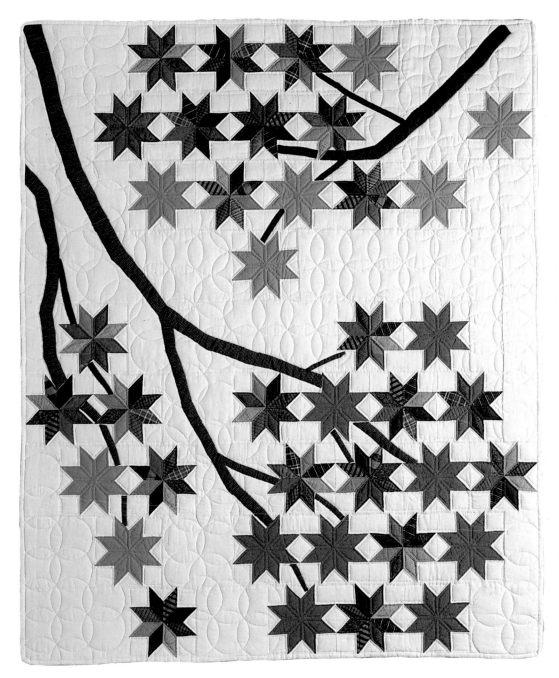

43. *Autumn Leaves* by Emiko Kosei, Takamatsu City, Kagawa Prefecture. 1985. 69″ x 60″ (175 x 153 cm).
Cotton crepes and cotton *tsumugi* (a closely woven slubbed fabric). Hand-pieced, appliquéd, and quilted.
The autumn colors in Japan are as rich and varied as they are in parts of the United States, and in this expressive
wall hanging the quiltmaker has not only captured the mellow coloring of the countryside but has also given
us an interesting illustration of an Oriental artistic convention known as "broken branch painting." As the name
suggests, the aim is to concentrate the eye on a single branch or two, leaving the viewer to imagine the rest of
the tree. "I made it for my autumn house decoration," Kosei says, demonstrating the delight the Japanese take
in celebrating the changing of the seasons. Because she wanted her quilt to look like a scroll painting, she did
not give it borders, as this would have destroyed the unexpressed continuum of this style of art. She used locally
made fabrics because, she says, "so many of these country-textiles are dying out, so I like to commemorate and
promote them in my quilts." This charming piece is a classic illustration of how an American pattern (LeMoyne
Star) is being used to illustrate a typical Japanese artistic principle—a hybrid quilt in every sense of the word.

Japanese Designs

Here we enter a different world and begin to see a true Japanese spirit emerging: quilts that illustrate how their makers are moving away from American patterns and influences and are starting to draw on their own traditional sources of design. You will find quilts that look like magnificent screen paintings, others that illustrate religious symbolism, or are inspired by some ancient handicraft, pastime, or festival.

The affection that the Japanese have for their beautiful textiles will also be evident from the way some quilt artists have arranged their designs so that the main interest is the fabric and not the pattern. In figure 44 we can see, for example, how the luminescence of patterned kimono silk emerges when worked in a simple design, and you will find other quilts in this section where large pieces of silk are framed in some simple setting, or flanked by piecework, and then elaborately quilted to throw the original hand-painted design into relief.

There is a wonderful variety of fabrics available to the quiltmaker in Japan: cottons, bast-fiber fabrics and, above all, silks. Much of this fabric is stencil-dyed in gorgeous colors, and Japanese quiltmakers buy up old kimono at flea markets, or acquire them from the

44. *Anvil* by Setsuko Takahashi, Yokohama. 1985. 71″ x 59″ (180 x 150 cm). Silk *kasuri* (an ikat-woven fabric). Hand-pieced and hand-quilted. In this beautiful piece you can see how the iridescence of kimono silk can illuminate an ordinary patchwork block. Takahashi made the quilt as a memorial to her father-in-law's silk business. The splash-patterned fabrics are a type of ikat that the Japanese call *kasuri*, a weaving technique that came to Japan originally from southeast Asia via Okinawa. Unfortunately, demand for these silk ikats declined after World War II, when women began to wear Western clothing and to prefer synthetic fabrics. "They were such lovely silks," Takahashi says, "and he had so many samples left that I decided to make them up into a quilt for him. He was very pleased with the result, and the rest of my family appreciated what I had tried to do for him, so you could say we all lived happily ever after!"

45. Naomi Itaya's wonderful collection of kimono silks has inspired her to take up patchwork again. She gave it up because she was finding it hard to create anything new, then one day she spied a shop selling pieces of old kimono, mostly the popular stencil-dyed silk crepes. "I was bowled over by their psychedelic coloring," she says. "It looked so fresh and new and, of course, this type of fabric is much easier to piece than fine silk." Since then Itaya has collected fabric mementos of her country's past: fabric-covered boxes, pouches, children's toys, even a patriotic memento of the Pacific War—a little cushion showing the flags of the three Axis powers—and, of course, kimono. You can see her sitting happily among her treasure trove with one of her new quilts made from kimono silks in the background.

cupboards of older relatives. The most popular fabric with quilters is silk crepe (*chirimen*), for its lively rippled surface and firm weave makes it easy to work with. In figure 45 Naomi Itaya sits in her Aladdin's cave of lovely silk crepes. A plentiful supply of strong handmade paper is the reason why Japan developed stencil-dyeing rather than block-printing, and dyeing therefore became one of the great Japanese textile arts.

The quilts illustrated in this chapter also express some of the fundamental principles of design that have governed the working of Japanese artists and craftsmen since ancient times. The Japanese love nature deeply and throughout the centuries they have arranged their homes, their ceremonies, and the decoration of their clothing so as to integrate the beauty of nature into their daily lives. The themes and coloring of Japanese quilts reflect this love.

An important part of Japanese design aims to achieve true purity and perfection through simplicity; consequently, simplification is a principle that is evident in many quilts. In this section and in others that follow, you will see how the rustic tends to be valued over the sophisticated and frugality over complexity.

You will also see how many quiltmakers prefer simplicity in their subject matter: a single flower rather than a bouquet; mountain peaks rather than a fully integrated landscape; a single motif to illustrate an annual children's festival. This approach is, of course, reflected in so much of Japanese life: from their small houses with the compact use of space, to the uncomplicated shape of the kimono, and to their exquisitely presented, but ultimately simple, food.

An important principle of Japanese design is asymmetry, and we have already seen in the first chapter how Japanese quiltmakers will try to introduce some element of irregularity to break up the constraint of a symmetrical design. This love for the vitality and movement of the irregular and oblique also comes from their identification with nature. In Japan, man is considered to be only a part of the natural world around him, and the ideal, therefore, is nature with all its irregularities and imperfections.

Natural themes, simplicity, and asymmetry are not new to quiltmakers, of course, but the Japanese have refreshing ways of combining them that may give you some new ideas for your own quilts.

46. *Clouds over Pine Trees* designed by Sanae Hattori and made by Etsuko Kawamura, Yokohama. 1984. 79″ x 79″ (200 x 200 cm). Cotton, silk, polyester, and synthetic lamé. Hand-pieced, some machine-piecing, embroidery, and hand-quilted. To introduce this section on Japanese designs, here is a quilt made by one of Japan's leading quiltmakers, who was among the first to combine traditional Japanese imagery with American patchwork methods. Hattori tells us that this exquisite design is her interpretation of the classic backdrop in Noh theatre, which is always a stylized pine tree set against gold, although the gold in this case takes the form of billowing clouds. Clouds are a traditional technique used by Oriental artists to separate areas of activity and provide a place to rest the eye. You find them on many screen paintings and handscrolls, and because genuine gold leaf comes in square pieces, Hattori has reflected this in the shape of her patches. Pine trees in Japan are usually symbolized in all forms of art by the stylized curved shape seen in this quilt, the shape being similar to the clusters of pine needles on a genuine tree, which Hattori designed in varied shades of green. Hattori studied embroidery at college, which opened her eyes to the wonderful patterns of her native land, and she established her own art studio soon after graduating, and now teaches patchwork to a large group of students. "I felt I wanted to use quilts to expand the horizons of Japanese design," she says. She has published two books: *The Quilt Japan* in 1985, followed by *Patchwork Quilts from Japanese Designs* in 1987. Her work has been widely exhibited in Japan and the U.S. Three of her quilts appeared in *Hands All Around*; one was chosen for the cover. Photograph courtesy the artist.

47. *Kirigami* by Naoko Izumisawa, Ashigarakami Gun, Kanagawa Prefecture. 1985. 66" across (168 cm). Kimono silks and cottons. Hand-pieced and quilted. The Japanese have a plentiful supply of handmade paper at their disposal and have therefore perfected two paper arts: *origami*, which is folding paper into bird, animal, and flower shapes; and *kirigami*, which you see here, that involves folding and cutting ornamental patterns. This outstanding work is a monument to the maker's patience and dexterity. Izumisawa wanted to create the effect of a spider's web ("and also the rising sun"), so having made a genuine paper-cut she then drew it to scale and used this to make her templates. She pieced wedges of kimono silks together to form the background and stitched these to the narrow orange wedges of the surface "web" (see details). The idea was to create circles revolving behind a paper-cut, although she says "you can see that my so-called circles turned out anything but circular!" She needed to disguise the unsightly ends so she appliquéd red half-circles over them, and you can see these on each side of the intersecting square frames, the only part of the quilt that is appliquéd. She created a contrast to the circular effect of the design by quilting it with squares radiating out from the center. This lovely piece is dedicated to her mother, who keeps her supplied with kimono silks. "I like to use fabric that belonged to people I know," she tells us. "That way I feel I am close to my friends and my family while I am working."

48. *Origami Crane* by Fumiko Fujita, Nagano City, Nagano Prefecture. 1985. 81″ x 63″ (205 x 160 cm). *Aizome* cottons and cotton sheeting. Hand-pieced, appliquéd, and quilted. The other traditional Japanese paper-craft, *origami*, which involves folding paper into bird and animal shapes without cutting is illustrated in this elegant quilt. You sometimes see three- or four-year-old Japanese children doing *origami* on the subway; good practice for nimble fingers. Fujita tells us that she had a fine collection of stencil-dyed fabrics and wanted to make something to decorate her Western-style living room. "It has white walls," she tells us, "and I didn't want anything too self-consciously Japanese." She took the crane pattern from a piece of wrapping paper and decided to combine it with a symmetrical pieced setting. Notice the clever way in which she has worked her light and dark fabrics to create the look of folded paper: each part of the little bird required a separate template, and she increased the authenticity by quilting down the center of each neck and tail. Fujita is the leader of a local quilt group, and this charming piece was hung in their 1985 exhibition and at Swiss Quilt '87 in Berne, Switzerland. "I think it looks happier in my living room," she says, "than floodlit in an exhibition hall."

49. *Iroha Characters* by Hisako Sakamoto, Tokyo. 1985. 55″ x 46″ (140 x 118 cm). Old blue jeans for the background; inner linings of old neckties and some woolen fabrics for the characters; a man's woolen kimono for the borders. Hand-pieced and appliquéd. As you can see from the list of materials used to make this vibrant wall hanging, Hisako Sakamoto believes in recycling the kind of leftovers most people throw away. She calls her work "Fabric Calligraphy," and in this striking quilt, assembled like a six-fold screen, she chose to illustrate an old way of learning one of the two Japanese phonetic syllabaries. The Japanese writing system is the most cumbersome in the world (learning it, however, does wonders for the brain!). Because their highly inflected spoken language was unsuited to the Chinese writing system that they "borrowed" in the fifth century A.D., the Japanese were obliged to invent two extra syllabaries based on simplified characters to modify word endings. The *iroha* method of the quilt's title was an old way of memorizing one of these syllabaries and it reads like a poem that translates as follows: "The colors blossom, scatter and fall./ In this world of ours, who lasts forever?/ Today let us cross over the remote mountains/ of life's illusions./ And dream no more shallow dreams nor/ succumb to drunkenness." Sakamoto also teaches traditional Japanese dancing, and owns a bakery business and a coffee shop where her patrons critique her work. "Their encouragement acts on me like a tonic," she says.

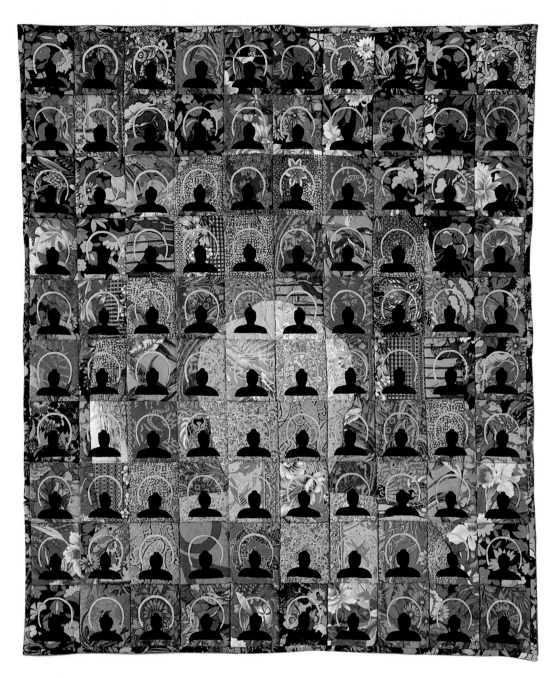

50. *A Thousand Buddhas in the Jungle* by Zero Arai, Omiga City, Saitama Prefecture. 1984. 59″ x 50″ (150 x 126 cm). Cotton prints. Reverse-appliqué. Inspired by photographs of Buddhist statuary buried in the junglè around Angkor Wat in Cambodia, Zero Arai had difficulty collecting the right kind of richly hued fabrics in Japan to create the effect she wanted for this outstanding Buddhist mandala. "I needed luxurious prints, alive with the kind of strong primary color you find in India and Tibet, but which don't exist here, so I had to find shops that sold export fabrics because they use a different palette from textiles produced for the home market. Friends helped me too, by giving me cottons they had bought overseas." A skilled quiltmaker of long-standing (known to her friends as the "Contest Wizard" because she has received so many awards), Arai expertly placed these exotic prints to set off the subtly toned and shaded figure of the Buddha in the center. Then she overlaid the entire piece with silhouetted images of the Buddha executed in reverse-appliqué. You will find similar representations of "A Thousand Buddhas" carved in stone, carved in wood, or painted on silk in temples and other holy places throughout Asia. As a god, the Buddha is able to manifest himself indefinitely, which mollified his early followers, who were afraid that just one incarnation of him might not be enough to help the millions who came to him for succor. (Buddhism and Shintoism are the two main religions in Japan.) Photograph courtesy Susumu Tomita.

51. *Abare Noshi* by Keiko Mori, Kobe City, Hyogo Prefecture. 1986. 83″ x 63″ (210 x 160 cm). Cotton prints and solid sheeting. Hand-pieced, appliquéd, and quilted. The flying ribbon motif on this vivid, contemporary-looking quilt is almost as old as Japan itself and is a good-luck talisman called a *noshi* that is affixed to presents given on auspicious occasions. Today, *noshi* are made from strips of paper (or are printed on the wrapping paper), but in the distant past the *noshi* strips were pounded from dried pieces of abalone, a food considered worthy to be offered to the gods. Knots have spiritual power in Asia; they unite lovers there just as they do in the West, but they can also seal off an area from evil, such as the knotted decorations that guard the doorways of Japanese homes during the New Year celebrations. (One enterprising Japanese sealed off an area outside his house with a symbolically knotted rope to stop people parking there—and it worked!) In time, the *noshi* motif was adapted for textiles, notably kimono, and is often seen today on the heavy padded outer robe of the traditional wedding outfit. When making the "ribbons" for her lovely design, Keiko Mori hand-pieced or appliquéd each one with a different pattern. "Patterns were used that are common to both American and Japanese culture," she explains. "I noticed that foreign quiltmakers were using our designs, so I took the pattern for my quilt from a Christmas card printed for the foreign market, and I used Japanese and American fabrics too." Mori learned quiltmaking from Sachiko Aragane, and a quilt made by her *sensei* ("teacher") is illustrated in figure 124.

52. *Kimono Crazy Quilt* by Kazuko Ogi, Gifu City, Gifu Prefecture. 1986. 59″ x 51″ (150 x 130 cm). Cottons and silks. Crazy patchwork and *sashiko*-quilting. A silk patchwork coat belonging to a famous sixteenth-century Japanese warlord (see fig. 6) captured the imagination of Kazuko Ogi, who decided to re-create this National Treasure for her own pleasure. "I have never seen the real coat," she tells us, "so I copied the patchwork design from a picture in an art-history book." She wanted to reproduce the effect of the old Chinese silks as closely as possible, so she used neckties, silk handkerchiefs, and even dyed old fabrics and re-created the textile designs with fabric paint. The patched pieces in the real coat are put together in panels separated by gold cord. Ogi used gold-colored bias tape instead ("and what a bother it was keeping this a uniform width throughout!"). The "coat" is not quilted, so Ogi anchored the three layers of fabric by *sashiko*-quilting the surrounding background with sprays of leaves. In the middle ages in Japan it was customary to give a man a patchwork coat like this one on the auspicious birthdays (sixty-six, seventy-seven, and eighty-eight), and such a coat often contained the same number of patches as his age.

53. *The Mountains Near My Home* by Noriko Yamaguchi, Matsuyama City, Ehime Prefecture. 1985. 99″ x 99″ (252 x 252 cm). Kimono silks, cotton prints, and obi silks for the borders. Crazy patchwork. "I love the mountainous scenery of Japan," says the maker of this remarkable abstract quilt (whose name Yamaguchi means "mountain gate"), "because mountains change their appearance all the time. They look different in the early morning, or at dusk, or when bathed in sunshine, or when washed by rain. I tried to create the effect of hazy early morning light shining on the mountains near my home, and though it was difficult controlling the colors so that I created the look of a mountain range, I enjoyed the challenge." Yamaguchi restricted her palette to greens, purples, and touches of ochre, and put the design together in ten panels separated by narrow strips of printed fabric similar in construction to the sixteenth-century "Crazy patchwork" coat in figure 6. The effect here, however, is that of a mountain view seen through the wood-barred window of a traditional Japanese home. Yamaguchi was taught quiltmaking by Sanae Hattori (see fig. 46). "I used to be a retiring sort of person," she tells us, "but working in a group has changed me. I am now much more positive and outgoing, and I enjoy meeting people. Quiltmaking changed my life." In this exquisitely worked scene she has demonstrated a masterful handling of color and form.

54. *The Bamboo Quilt* by Naoko Hirai, Matsuyama City, Ehime Prefecture. 1985. 38″ x 51″ (96 x 130 cm). Kimono silks. Hand-appliquéd, string-pieced, and quilted. Naoko Hirai wanted to make a wall hanging that would harmonize with her traditional Japanese home, so the inspiration for this elegant quilt is a bamboo forest near the ancient capital city of Kyoto. "I love the fresh green of young bamboo, so I tried to create the effect of early morning light gleaming on the leaves and on my clamshell hills." Hirai tells us that she used to work only with calico prints and indigo cottons, but she now loves the effects she can obtain with silks. She collected as many different greens and pinks from temple fairs and flea markets to add to the collection of silks she had been given by her family. Hirai wears kimono, so she framed her delicately appliquéd landscape with a strong border of diagonally pieced kimono silks. She is another Japanese who says that quiltmaking is a wonderful way of making friends, "and it is also a challenge to my creativity."

55. *Hanafuda Quilt* by Setsuko Ideta, Kitaamabe Gun, Oita Prefecture. 1984. 73″ x 57″ (186 x 148 cm). Cotton sheeting. Hand-appliquéd, embroidered, and quilted. When she was planning a quilt to give her son for his fourteenth birthday, Setsuko Ideta hit upon the idea of re-creating a popular card game traditionally played by Japanese at New Year. Known as *hanafuda* ("flower cards"), the game is played with a forty-eight-card deck divided into twelve four-card suits. Each of these suits represents a different month of the year symbolized by a flower, a shrub, or a tree, some of which Ideta has meticulously reproduced in this unusual quilt. "It was great fun to make," she tells us, "because my son took such an interest, and we used to play around rearranging the quilt images when he got home from school." (Ideta's son's name, Jun, is embroidered in lavender in the top right corner of the border.) The colors used are mostly those of the actual playing cards: the mellow brown of the sashing, for example, can be found on the edges of each card. Ideta says, however, that she cheated a little when she realized that some of the card colors were too bright or did not blend in well with the others, and so she dyed some of the fabrics herself. One of her other quilts won "Best of Show" in a major regional exhibition.

56. *Japanese Decorative Plate* by Yoko Mizuno, Toki City, Gifu Prefecture. 1987. 52″ x 52″ (132 x 132 cm). Cotton prints, hand-dyed solids, kimono silks. Hand-pieced, quilted, and shadow-quilted. The centerpiece of this elegant quilt commemorates a famous type of Japanese pottery called *shino* ware that is used for teabowls used in the traditional tea ceremony. "I like the idea of exploring images of my country through quiltmaking," Mizuno tells us, "and *shino* ware is our local industry." She chose a plate with an unusually detailed design of a spray of spiraea; unusual because *shino* ceramics are usually decorated with simple impressionistic grasses or leaves. "The spiraea blossoms are like tiny white balls," she says, "and each one is a slightly different shape, so I tried to simulate this by making individual templates for each flower." In order to create the effect of underglaze painting, Mizuno cleverly shadow-quilted the center medallion by overlaying it with organdy. Because Mizuno likes to mix old and new fabrics, the vibrant, patched border is made from kimono silks and a Hawaiian cotton *muumuu*. This is Mizuno's second quilt on a ceramic theme; an earlier one depicted a coffee cup. Twenty years ago Mizuno made a patchwork quilt without really knowing how to do it. Then she joined a group and now says "quiltmaking gives a change of pace to my life."

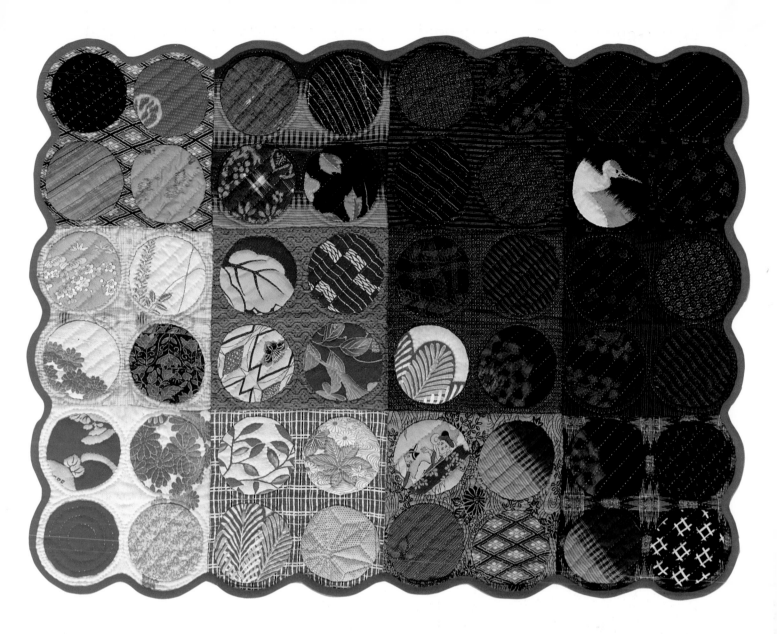

57. *The Dawn* by Reiko Shishikura, Makuhari City, Chiba Prefecture. 1985. 22″ x 30″ (57 x 77 cm). Kimono silks and cotton prints. Hand appliquéd and quilted. This exquisite little quilt with its 3″ (7.5 cm) circular blocks superbly graduated to create the effect of dawning light was made from fabrics given to Shishikura by her mother-in-law. "She died before the quilt was finished, and because she was such a great needlewoman (she was making her own kimono until she was well into her eighties) I dedicated it to her," Shishikura tells us. "Her name was Tsuru, which means 'crane' in Japanese, so I found a piece of fabric printed with a crane to illuminate the 'night' part of the quilt." The setting came from a quilt that Shishikura saw in an American magazine, but the symbolism behind the title is purely Japanese. As is the custom in Japan, her mother-in-law lived with Shishikura and her husband, which meant that after she died Shishikura's life changed completely. The 'dawn' symbolizes a new beginning for me," she says. "There was pain and pleasure in making this quilt. Pain in trying to create the effect of dawning light from the limited fabrics I had at my disposal, and pleasure in quilting along the patterns of these lovely old pieces. We found them stored away when we rebuilt the family home to accommodate us all." Shishikura teaches, and one of her quilts won "Best of Show" in an interior-design contest.

58. *The Beauty of Silk* by Yoshiko Ogawa, Higashimurayama City, Tokyo. 1984. 80″ x 80″ (204 x 204 cm). Kimono and obi silks. Hand-pieced and quilted. The unusual setting of this beautifully planned quilt illustrates how Japanese quiltmakers like to show off their traditional fabrics to the best advantage. "In the early 1980s, old kimono and obi were very cheap (not like today) and I wanted to give new life to these lovely old silks," says Ogawa, "so I framed a center panel made of hand-painted obi silk with two side panels of variegated piecework." The large pieces at the top left and bottom right were cut from the lining of a man's coat (a traditional *haori* worn over kimono). Clothing regulations in Japan's past forbade commoners to wear luxury silks, which prompted rich merchants to line drab outer garments with these forbidden fabrics. Landscapes, such as you see here, were very respectable, but as a witty form of protest (and to create a sensation at parties), a fantastic array of other linings were invented: painted skulls, ghosts, cards, dice, or even pornography (it is still possible to buy men's second hand *haori*, with female nudes painted on the lining). "I enjoyed these large pieces because I could quilt freely," Ogawa tells us, "but quilting silk is difficult because it is so slippery. In the seven years that I have been making quilts I have certainly learned patience!" Ogawa runs a group of seventy quilters and arranges an exhibition every two years for which she specifies a theme such as "Japan," which was the inspiration for this quilt.

59. *Hien* ("Secret Fire") by Emiko Toda Loeb, New York City. 1987. 89″ x 67″ (226 x 170 cm). *Aizome* cottons, cotton prints, and antique silks. Hand-pieced, machine-pieced, hand-quilted. The glowing reds of the randomly pieced background in this majestic work reflects the quilt's title. "I wanted to make a quilt where traditional patterns could be worked in and around free-flowing lines and shapes; something both traditional and abstract," the artist tells us. The great sweep of gray flowing like a river down the surface is probably the quilt's most traditional Japanese element: you find representations of water similarly cascading down the back of seventeenth-century kimono. For the striking blue intersecting column Loeb has used an ancient Japanese pattern, a stylized hemp leaf, while the river is worked with a traditional bobbin shape. "Each of these large sections was assembled first, usually in strips, and then joined to the background later," Loeb explains. "I bought most of the fabrics from flea markets in Kyoto, but some are really old pieces, heirlooms you might call them, more than a hundred years old, that were given to me by friends." Loeb's imaginative quilts have a universal appeal, but their inspiration and design reflect her Japanese heritage. Two other quilts made by this artist are illustrated in figures 23, 23a, and 88. *Hien* appeared in the February 1988 issue of *Quilter's Newsletter Magazine*. Photograph courtesy the artist.

60. *Sayagata Medallion* by Yoko Narita, Koriyama City, Fukushima Prefecture. 1984. 67″ x 67″ (170 x 170 cm). Japanese sheeting. Hand-appliquéd and quilted. As the theme of her group's exhibition in 1984 was to be "Japanese Designs," Narita made this striking appliqué quilt in just three months. She chose a complex key-fret motif for her central medallion that is probably Japan's best-loved pattern: the *sayagata* of the title. It is an ancient design that came to Japan from China, and you find it today as a woven pattern in kimono silks, painted on porcelain, and resist-dyed on *yukata* cottons. It is also a very popular *sashiko* grid. Narita tells us that she thoroughly enjoyed the discipline of appliquéing this mazelike pattern, but says, "I was so surprised how contemporary and Western my quilt looked after I added the borders of circles and squares, not at all what I had intended!" (Note carefully how she has altered the patterns on the left and right and top and bottom inner border.) She went to considerable trouble to find a particular grayed shade of purple, which is indelibly associated in the Japanese mind with kimono, in order to soften the strong graphic effect. "Then I tried to bring back the Japanese flavor by quilting these borders with some of our family crest motifs."

61. *Kagome* ("Basketweave") by Keiko Minato, Hiroshima. 1986. 34″ x 29″ (86 x 74 cm). Kimono silks and cotton voile. Hand-pieced and quilted. The variegated flowers and decorative silken balls appearing on the central hexagons of this pretty crib quilt are typical patterns used for children's kimono. Whenever Minato comes across old kimono fabrics, she likes to learn their history so that she can design an appropriate quilt. This particular multipatterned silk was cut from the kimono that was used to wrap her neighbor's baby when she was taken to the family shrine for a traditional blessing soon after she was born. "She was such a darling baby," reminisces Minato, "that I had to make the prettiest quilt I could and dedicate it to her. I used double-thickness batting to make it puffy and set my hexagons with cream and white borders." Red and white are typical celebratory colors in Japan—fresh and festive, recalling the clear colors of the early-morning sun. Minato's mother was a seamstress, so she grew up with kimono silks and cottons and was using them for her quilts long before they became fashionable with other Japanese quiltmakers. "When I sew, I feel I am communicating with all the people involved in these lovely old fabrics. Not only their original owners, but the weavers and dyers too." Minato also made the *Furoshiki Mola Quilt* in "Country Textiles" (fig. 116).

62. *Gliding Geese* by Sawako Tsurugiji, Kanazawa City, Ishikawa Prefecture. 1984. 42″ x 57″ (106 x 145 cm). Kimono and obi silks. Hand-pieced and quilted. Japanese quiltmakers often prefer to let their traditional fabrics speak for themselves, and in this charming wall hanging Tsurugiji has framed two panels cut from an embroidered obi with simple piecework in order to emphasize the fine work in the panels. "It is customary to wear kimono and obi that are appropriate for the season, so this obi would have been worn in the autumn," she tells us. "The embroidered geese are an autumn motif, for it is at this season that they glide and play over the lakes of Japan before settling down for the winter." Tsurugiji has used trapunto to enhance the flowing curves of the water and then did parallel quilting in the background to throw the water and birds into relief. She explains that it was a love of antiques that led her into quiltmaking originally. Her hometown of Kanazawa is one of the few Japanese cities that has many samurai houses still standing (it is called "Little Kyoto"), and it is in an area particularly rich in Japanese history and culture. "I found such lovely old fabrics in the antiques shops, and I wanted to bring them to life again in something new." Most of her early quilts were made with indigo-dyed cottons (see her quilt *Windmills* illustrated in figure 107), but now she enjoys working with these beautiful old kimono silks.

63. *Rainbow Quilt* by Mikoko Hashimoto, Hakodate City, Hokkaido. 1984. 81″ x 68″ (206 x 174 cm). Cambric, broadcloth, sheeting. Hand-pieced and quilted. The Japanese love graduated color; you can see this from the way they arrange the coloring of the various layers of kimono to give a pleasing arrangement at the neckline. In ancient times, the imperial courtiers wore fifteen or twenty layers of robes, and each one was dyed a shade or two paler than the last. "I wanted to make one original quilt in my life," says the maker of this magnificent essay in graduated color. "At first I tried to do a quilt entirely in blues, to represent the curves of a river because I like anything to do with water, but I had to abandon it because I found one color too limiting, so I switched to a rainbow palette." She complicated her task by limiting herself to commercial fabrics ("I didn't want to get into dyeing cloth myself"). She begged from all her friends and haunted the fabric shops in the city. "I even cut the solid parts from printed cottons to get the tone I wanted," she says, "and as I was making the quilt for our group exhibition, I had to work eighteen hours a day at times in order to meet the deadline. I also sewed several of the blocks over and over, because what seemed like a perfect color sequence at night looked disastrous next morning!" Despite its size the quilt was finished on time (it took her two and a half months), and was exhibited at the *Swiss Quilt '86* exhibition in Berne, Switzerland.

64. *Shaded Dawn* by Toshiko Uchiyama, Inba Gun, Chiba Prefecture. 1983. 50″ x 70″ (128 x 177 cm). Synthetic lining fabrics. English piecework, appliqué, embroidery, and quilting. Here is a quilter who has dared to use synthetic fabrics to make her exquisite mountain landscape ("I was a novice and didn't know any better!"). She wanted to enter a national needlework contest that had "Morning" as its theme, but had no idea how to make a quilt. "I'm a dressmaker by trade, and because I wanted my entry to have a proper Japanese feeling I used synthetic lining fabric, which looks and gleams like silk, leftover from my work." Uchiyama used the English method of piecing over papers in order to keep her pattern accurate, but even this method caused headaches. "Synthetics won't take a crease and fray badly, so I had to paste all 2,400 of my fabric patches to the papers before I could even baste down the edges. Then I had to unpick and resew numerous patches to get the right perspective." Her dedication and determination were rewarded. The quilt is a perfect evocation of early morning light spreading across the mountainous scenery of Japan. She has either embroidered or quilted stylized trees in the upright triangles in the foreground mountain to represent the lush forests that clothe Japanese mountainsides. The design was inspired by a modern painting. "I didn't win a prize," Uchiyama says, "but every stitch was an adventure."

65. *Kimono Quilt* by Shizue Takagi, Kyoto. 1986. 67″ x 37″ (170 x 95 cm). Cotton broadcloth and kimono silks. Hand-appliquéd, clamshell- and *sashiko*-quilted. Shizue Takagi made this sampler quilt with its unusual S-shaped setting of multilined silk clamshells in memory of her mother. "I have been collecting leftover pieces from my family's traditional clothing for ages," she says, "and I wanted to recycle them in some creative or artistic way. The quilt was made in memory of my mother." The quilt is a sampler in the true sense of the word, for each little kimono is made from a different dyed or woven kimono fabric. "I make my own kimono so I am accustomed to working with silk," Takagi tells us. "My greatest pleasure in life nowadays is making quilts because I feel I am using my time constructively, and quiltmaking is also a way of prolonging the life of our lovely traditional fabrics." Takagi quilted the alternate blocks with a simple plum-blossom motif, and completed her borders by *sashiko*-quilting them in a grid, except for the bottom left corner, where she added a delightful touch by finishing off with a few echo-quilted clamshells.

66. *Flower Calendar* by Yuko Yamamoto, Oita City, Oita Prefecture. 1986. 77″ x 61″ (195 x 155 cm). Cotton prints, solid Japanese sheeting, new and old *aizome* cottons. Appliquéd, embroidered, and quilted, Crazy-patched borders. The Japanese year is punctuated by festivals and ceremonies, many of which are associated with flowers: cherry blossom-viewing in April, iris-viewing in June, and expeditions to enjoy autumn coloring in early November, which is every bit as spectacular as in parts of the United States. Therefore, to introduce this small section of commemorative quilts, we thought a traditional flower calendar would be appropriate. Yamamoto took the patterns for this fresh and dainty quilt from a book of kimono designs, but she changed some of the seasonal flowers to others more to her liking. The calendar starts at top left, with narcissus for January, plum blossom for February (also an unofficial "flower-viewing" ceremony), violet for March, and ends with a spray of nanten (at bottom right), which is often used as a symbol of a faithful wife because the red berries cling to the stem all through the hardships of winter. The quilt's borders—Crazy-patched on three sides and quilted on the fourth—arrests the eye. This unorthodox treatment successfully breaks the monotony of having all the borders handled alike: a typical Japanese touch. Yamamoto framed her blocks with narrow strips of antique *aizome* and has embroidered the name of the flower in each block.

67. *New Year's Quilt* by Miyoko Yano, Kasugai City, Aichi Prefecture. 1986. 37″ x 24″ (93 x 62 cm). Cotton *futon* fabric, vegetable-dyed cottons. Hand-pieced, appliquéd, and quilted. Japanese kites are among the most spectacular in the world, and it is customary to fly them on New Year's Day in deference to the past when the ancients used kites to carry prayers for good fortune up to the gods. Among the many designs kitemakers paint on these classic examples of Japanese folk art are images taken from popular woodblock prints, notably those of *kabuki* actors. When Yano found some *futon* fabric printed with *kabuki* kites, she decided to use it to make a quilt for family New Year festivities. She adapted the American Drunkard's Path pattern to create a flight of birds "soaring in the air with the kites." Being a perfectionist and unable to find cotton of the right color tone to match the old *futon* fabric, Yano made dye colors from safflowers, chrysanthemums, and onion skins and then dyed new cotton herself. Her contour-quilting combined with the soft shading of the background fabric gives us a kite's-eye view of the barren fields of winter. Yano has included a promise of spring in the scattered plum blossoms at the bottom. Branches of plum blossom are a feature in the traditional Japanese New Year decorations. Yano has another interesting quilt illustrated in figure 113.

68. *Kabuki Kite* by Akemi Kura, Fukuyama City, Hiroshima Prefecture. 1986. 39″ x 30″ (98 x 75 cm). Cotton, organdy, and kimono fabrics. Stained-glass technique, reverse-appliqué, and appliqué. Kites came to Japan originally from China where, as well as operating as a form of spiritual telegraph (see fig. 67), they were also used by the military for signaling. Perhaps in memory of this, it became fashionable in the eighteenth century to decorate kites with the fierce, scowling faces of warriors taken from traditional woodblock prints. These martial "samurai kites" are now associated with the New Year's festivities. "I thought it would be interesting to make a quilt like one of these little paper kites," Kura explains, "and I even mounted my quilt on bamboo stretchers like the real thing." She faithfully copied the design and coloring of a kite she had bought, using a variety of different techniques, but says she had difficulty in getting the facial expression right. ("I have to admit that the bit I liked best in the whole project was the very last stitch!") Although not particularly drawn to Japanese things, Kura says she is constantly surprised how fresh and original Japanese designs are. Her masterly interpretation of this traditional piece of Japanese folk craft makes this a most unusual quilt. Kura is self-taught and has had a solo exhibition in Fukuyama City.

69. *Dolls' Festival* by Rieko Hattori, Kawasaki City, Kanagawa Prefecture. 1983. 14″ x 14″ (36 x 36 cm). Silk, cotton, felt, and beads. Hand-pieced, appliquéd, and quilted. This is another of Hattori's charming miniature quilts (see figs. 34, 71), and the symbolism behind this one is the Girls' Festival celebrated each year on March 3 (not a public holiday as is Boys' Day). Dolls and peach blossoms are associated with this festival; dolls because the festival is based on an ancient purification rite, during which families threw paper dolls in the local river in the hopes that they would carry away with them all the possible illnesses and misfortunes of the coming year. Today, little girls are given a set of *hina* dolls magnificently dressed in the style of the ancient imperial court (see fig. 70), which they arrange on a tiered stand, and folklore conveniently says that if the dolls are not put away immediately after the festival by their owner she will remain an old maid! Hattori made this charming quilt for her two daughters and tried to create the feeling of a hazy spring morning; the white silk shapes in the background are a familiar Japanese stylization of mist. Peach blossoms are associated with this festival because this is the time of year when the peach tree blooms, and Hattori made her delicately colored blossoms three-dimensional. The boldly striped borders are another traditional touch. The ceremonial *hina* dolls in a Japanese home sit on miniature versions of the customary tatami mats, which are edged with colorful striped bindings just as you see here. Photograph courtesy Susumu Tomita.

70. *Hina Dolls* by Yoko Takei, Maebashi City, Gunma Prefecture. 1985. 22″ x 16″ (55 x 41 cm). Cotton and ramie. Hand-pieced and quilted. A brief explanation of Japanese court costume is necessary if the subject matter of this ingenious miniquilt is to be appreciated. As we saw in the previous quilt, it is the custom for young girls to be given a set of dolls (the *hina* dolls of the title) dressed in the elaborate court clothing of feudal Japan with which to celebrate their annual festival on March 3. In those days, ladies of the court wore an astonishing number of robes, one on top of another (sometimes as many as twenty), which were colored so as to create an artistic, layered effect at the neck, sleeve edges, and hem. The outfit was topped by a cloak of rich brocade, and underneath it all the courtiers wore a padded red divided skirt that gave them a somewhat triangular silhouette. (You can see this clearly in the *hina* doll in figure 69.) They wore long black hair hanging loose, and they carried fans. When Takei was planning her quilt, she decided to show a human figure in patchwork—"something original, something humorous, something Japanese." She says that Japanese toys exert a strange fascination for her "probably because of their long history." But she likes to upgrade traditional designs by showing them in a modern setting so she designed a patchwork block based on one of these courtly dolls. "The image is of a group of court ladies gossiping," she tells us. This unusual and lively work won second prize in a competition organized by *Patchwork Quilt Tsūshin*.

71. *Boys' Day* by Rieko Hattori. Kawasaki City, Kanagawa Prefecture. 1984. 15″ x 15″ (39 x 39 cm). Cotton, sateen, and ornamental cord. Hand-pieced and quilted. "Most quilts are made for girls," says Hattori, "so having made several for my daughters, I thought I would commemorate the Boys' Day that is celebrated each year on May 5. Just as the Girls' Festival is marked by displays of elaborately costumed dolls, so is Boys' Day marked with sets of miniature samurai armor, or armor-clad dolls representing famous Japanese heroes." To a Westerner the unlikely combination of a samurai helmet surrounded by irises may seem incongruous, but it is in fact traditional. In the old days, May 5 was the Iris Festival when people hung bunches of iris under the eaves of their houses to ward off evil spirits. Floating iris leaves in the bath was also supposed to keep disease at bay for a year. Although the modern iris seems to flower later—the festival now takes place in June—the two remain associated for Boys' Day, partly because of old associations and partly because the Japanese word for "iris" sounds the same as the word for "brave." Hattori drew up her own pattern for the helmet but the irises are an adaptation of an old Ruby McKim design. Each of these charming festival quilts took Hattori four weeks to make. Photograph courtesy Susumu Tomita.

72. *Carp Quilt* by Keiko Nakamura, Tokyo. 1986. 58″ x 45″ (148 x 114 cm). Printed cotton, shirt fabrics. Hand-pieced, appliquéd, and quilted. Although carp are traditionally associated with Boys' Day (huge carp-shaped windsocks are flown over the roofs of Japanese houses), Keiko Nakamura made this quilt for her husband. "Carp are associated with masculinity," she explains, "because they swim upstream jumping cataracts, and Chinese legend says that once they have successfully negotiated the cataracts they turn into dragons: tough, brave, and fearless—all manly virtues! My husband is mad about carp: he keeps them in a pond in our garden and collects calendars illustrated with carp; so when I found I had a number of his old shirts, I decided to make a quilt for him using the subtle stripes of the fabrics to create the effect of a waterfall." For the carp itself ("my daughter helped me a lot with this"), Nakamura used some of her precious scraps of antique *aizome* and *yukata* fabrics, but she bought the printed *sashiko* fabric for the border. "I don't think Japanese designs have to be made with Japanese fabrics, but I must confess I do look at kimono shops to get ideas about color." The flick of red in the carp's eye, echoed in the narrow red inner border, adds a distinctive touch to this graphic fabric painting. Nakamura is self-taught, and another of her quilts with a Japanese theme appears in figure 129.

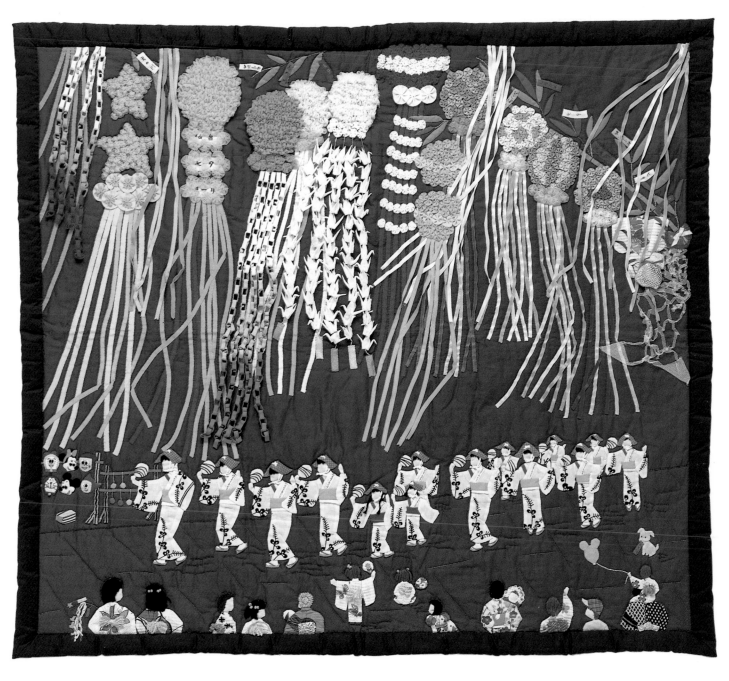

73. *When I Wish Upon a Star* by Kouko Nishizawa, Sendai City, Miyagi Prefecture. 1984. 43″ x 49″ (110 x 124 cm). Cotton, organdy, and multicolored ribbons. Hand-appliquéd and quilted. This wonderfully eye-catching quilt is an illustration of one of Japan's five important annual festivals: *Tanabata*, held on July 7, a festival that celebrates the only night of the year when two stars, Vega and Altair, can be seen together in the night sky. According to Chinese legend, Vega was a weaver who neglected her heavenly duties because of her love for the herdsman, Altair. To punish them, the Emperor of Heaven banished them to the opposite ends of the Milky Way and allowed them to meet once a year, weather permitting. If the sky is cloudy, then the lovers are doomed to wait for another twelve months, but not, fortunately, the festival. *Tanabata* is celebrated all over Japan, rain or shine, and the decorations range from simple sprays of bamboo hung with poems written on strips of paper to the kind of lavish decorations shown on this quilt. The northern city of Sendai, where Nishizawa was born, is one of the two places in Japan that is noted for its elaborate *Tanabata* celebrations. The quilt is a masterpiece of ingenuity. Nishizawa has pleated and folded fabric to create a vivid three-dimensional effect. The giant balls of flowers, which are plastic in real life, are ribbon yo-yos, and the streamers of *origami* cranes are as accurate as if they had been folded from paper. Each hat-string and obi sash is knotted, and the patterns on the dancers' fans and kimono are made to scale. Nishizawa has set her memorable scene against the dark blue of a night sky to honor the nocturnal lovers.

74. *Sakura* ("Cherry Blossoms") by Miwako Kimura, Tokyo. 1988. 54″ x 78″ (136 x 198 cm). Old indigo-dyed cottons, old kimono silks, hand-dyed new cotton. Hand-pieced, appliquéd, quilted, and *sashiko*-quilted. The most celebrated Japanese festival is, of course, the one for cherry-blossom viewing, which takes place each year in April. The maker of this exquisite quilt says, "Every artist's creativity is affected when they see Japanese cherry trees reflected in water, and so was I." Miwako Kimura is fascinated by the designs of her native land (her *kamon* quilt is illustrated in fig. 125), and in this wonderful piece she has combined a number of significant Japanese patterns and symbols. Moon-viewing is also a popular pastime in Japan, and because it is customary to celebrate the arrival of the cherry blossoms by drinking sake under the trees at night, Kimura has included a moon in her quilt. It is seen here partially concealed by the cloud of fragile blossoms ("some are made from the collar of an underkimono my mother bought me when I was ten") and by stylized strands of mist. A curious feature of moon-viewing festivals is that the Japanese often choose to contemplate the moon two or three days before it is full. "The moon is always more beautiful before it is completely round," Kimura explains. This is yet another instance of the Japanese affection for irregularity. Water is represented in the quilt by a swirling cascade of appliqué and quilting. Basketweave patterns are also associated with water in Japan because of the custom of shoring up crumbling river banks with bamboo baskets filled with pebbles. The check pattern pieced with various traditional fabrics is known as *ishidatami*, meaning "paving stones." Because this beautiful piece is so quintessentially Japanese we chose it for the cover of this book. Photograph courtesy Ryuta Kimura.

75. *Seven Grasses of Autumn* by Yasuko Kato, Shimada City, Shizuoka Prefecture. 1984. 70″ x 43″ (178 x 108 cm). Hand-dyed sheeting, ribbons. Hand string-piecing, hand-appliqué, embroidery, and quilting. This Festival quilt celebrates *Tsukimi*, the moon-viewing festival that takes place in September at the autumn equinox. Kato is a dressmaker by profession, and on her way home each night she passes a little river where the wild flowers are particularly lovely in the autumn, so she decided to capture this tranquil scene for her entry in the local cultural fair. "I paint with my fabric using my needle as a brush," she tells us. The "Seven Grasses" of the quilt's title are a popular decorative combination (ingeniously embroidered here or else fashioned with silk ribbons) that also include flowers: bush clover, wild carnations, maiden flowers (the yellow ones with heads like open parasols), hemp agrimony, arrowroot, blue bellflowers, and pampas. In China and Japan there is not a "man in the moon," but a hare or a rabbit. In China, the hare spends its nights manufacturing the elixir of immortality, but the Japanese rabbit is a much more practical animal. As you can see in this appealing quilt, its job is to pound the rice to make the glutinous rice cakes traditionally eaten at this season. Kato says, "I sew for a living, but I wish I had more time to make quilts for myself."

Blue-and-White Quilts

It is the traditional Japanese indigo-dyed blue-and-white fabrics that unite the quilts we have selected for this section.

Japanese quiltmakers first began putting their national stamp on the foreign art of quiltmaking by using their lovely indigo-dyed fabrics. As a consequence, there are many "hybrids" illustrated here, for it was the "blue-and-white quilts" that consummated the marriage of American style with Japanese interpretation. One visionary artist who has made this field her own is Shizuko Kuroha, and her pioneering work has led to a school of blue-and-white quilts that have a unique Japanese essence (figs. 76, 77).

Blue and white, of course, has been a traditional color combination for centuries. Long after the porcelain industry developed richly colored underglaze-painting techniques, it was the simple blue-and-white ware that continued (and still continues) to delight the Japanese (fig. 78). Interestingly, much of the porcelain made in Japan often uses textile patterns in its decoration.

The origin of blue-and-white textiles lies in the past, when indigo was the easiest dye to obtain. Blue and white as a decorative combination really came into its own after cotton was introduced from China. Instead of stiff cumbrous fabrics made from hemp or layers or other bast-fiber fabrics with poor insulating qualities, light warm clothing became available when cotton cultivation spread during the eighteenth century. In its way, cotton was a kind of liberator, almost like a revolution, and it evaded the government clothing restrictions designed to enforce class divisions and Confucian frugality. Farmers, fishermen, merchants, and artisans, who were forbidden to wear the patterned silks and brocades restricted to the ruling classes, created wonderfully decorative dyeing methods that have made these simple cotton fabrics highly valued in Japan today.

Every village had its own dye-shop. Some dyed yarn for the housewife to weave at home herself, while others specialized in stencil-dyeing prewoven cloth (figs. 79–82). The first type of dyeing included the popular *kasuri*, a Japanese form of ikat weaving that was generally used for work clothing. The *kasuri* process involves binding sections of the warp and weft threads in some predetermined pattern and "reserving" them from the indigo dye so that when weaving commences these "reserved" areas formed the pattern. The blurred outlines of *kasuri* weaving gives these fabrics a magical quality exploited to the full by modern quiltmakers.

In the stencil-dyeing process, sturdy paper stencils were cut with intricate patterns and used to dye cotton fabric that the housewife made up into bedding, ornamental cloths for her furniture, and wrapping cloths like *furoshiki*, a square fabric carryall the Japanese traditionally use instead of a shopping bag. These stencil-dyed fabrics are now called *aizome*, although strictly speaking, this is a generic term that should cover all indigo-dyed cloth (it means "indigo-dyeing") including another popular rural technique called *tsutsugaki*. This technique involved drawing patterns—often elaborate pictures, family crests, or simple rustic designs—with a cone filled with rice paste and handled in a manner similar to frosting a cake. The lines of paste formed a resist against the penetration of the dye and when washed out of the fabric left the design revealed in the original color of the cloth. The magnificent kimono-shaped *futon* cover illustrated in figure 1 shows the wonderful creative effects that these rural craftsmen were able to achieve.

76. *Cosmos* by Shizuko Kuroha, Tokyo. 1983. 83″ x 63″ (210 x 160 cm). Antique *aizome* prints, striped and solid indigo-dyed cotton. Hand-pieced and quilted. This remarkable quilt, based on a computer graphic, was made by Shizuko Kuroha, who pioneered the idea of using traditional indigo-dyed fabrics and subsequently founded a group of talented quiltmakers whose "blue-and-white" quilts have been an inspiration to others. Kuroha took up quiltmaking in 1975, when she lived in the United States, but it was only after she had returned to Japan, where nobody kept a stock of American calicoes in those days, that she thought of using these old blue-and-white fabrics as an alternative. "I am careful to keep my work looking as clean and crisp as possible," she says, "because quilts made with antique *aizome* cottons can sometimes look really dirty. Nobody washed these fabrics in the old days." Her ingenious placement of color and the subtle gradations she has managed to achieve with these country-style fabrics make this quilt a fascinating work of art. Kuroha arranged an exhibition of her circle's work in New York in 1985 where the blue-and-white quilts created quite a stir. This particular quilt has been widely exhibited, and it has appeared in several publications, including the 1987 edition of *The Quilt Engagement Calendar*. Kuroha has published two books of her work. Photograph courtesy the artist.

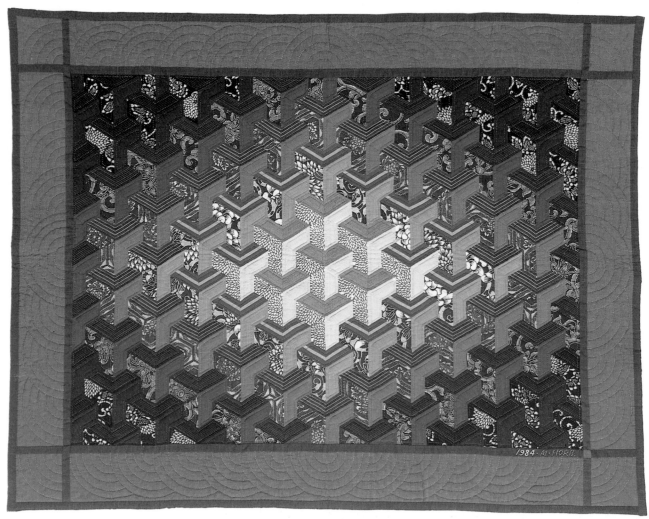

77. *Inner City Illuminated* by Mayumi Horii, Inashiki, Ibaraki Prefecture. 1984. 45″ x 59″ (115 x 150 cm). *Aizome* prints and cotton *tsumugi*. "I had always wanted to make a quilt like Jinny Beyer's *Inner City* but in Japanese fabrics," explains the maker of this striking piece. "I had a fine collection of *aizome* cottons that I had either bought in street markets or had been given by farmers in our neighborhood, and also some striped cotton that I wanted to use in an effective way." Her use of these stripes to underscore each block and the placement of light-colored fabrics to create the "illumination" in the center impart an unusual dynamism to this Japanese interpretation of Jinny Beyer's well-known design. "The way everything just fell into place was just like magic," Horii says. She is a former student of Shizuko Kuroha.

78. Blue-and-white porcelain is set off here with a fine piece of indigo-dyed cloth. The five little white cranes on the left are chopstick rests. All the items come from Hiroko Kawahito's collection of crane-patterned objects. Her *Crane Sampler* is illustrated in figure 83. Photograph courtesy Yuko Watanabe.

79, 80, 81, 82. The preparation of indigo is a long process and great skill is needed to achieve a satisfactory dye. The depth color is created by repeated dippings in the dye-bath. Indigo oxidizes in the fresh air. Shikoku is the traditional home of indigo-dyeing in Japan. Photographs courtesy Yuko Watanabe.

83. *Crane Sampler* by Hiroko Kawahito, Kanonji City, Kagawa Prefecture. 1984. 66″ x 45″ (168 x 114 cm). A variety of old and new resist-dyed cottons. Hand-pieced sashing and borders, hand-quilted. This elegant quilt with its varied tones of blue is a witness to the skills of Japan's rural craftsmen. Here we find illustrations of all the lovely old traditional methods of dyeing: *kasuri*, stencil-dyeing, and the more spontaneous *tsutsugaki*. The maker collects crane patterns (you can see some of her crane-patterned china in fig. 78), and she tells us that she does so because the logo of her family's sake-brewing business is a crane. In the quilt, the realistic-looking cranes are *kasuri*-woven, and the two *origami* cranes (fourth block down on the right) are of the *tsutsugaki* type. The more elaborate crane patterns are all stencil-dyed. Another of Kawahito's intriguing crane quilts is illustrated in figure 126, and a third appeared in *Hands All Around*. She runs a quilt group in her hometown.

84. *A Maze* by Ritsuko Takahashi, Tokyo. 1984. 80″ x 70″ (203 x 178 cm). Old *aizome, kasuri,* and hand-dyed cotton. Hand-pieced and quilted. In this diverting quilt Ritsuko Takahashi has turned the familiar Drunkard's Path pattern inside out and made the background the strongest feature of the design. "I love this pattern," she tells us, "because my own life is a bit like a drunkard's path!" She made each block individually, using favorite pieces from her collection of indigo-dyed fabrics, and set them together so that the multipatterned blocks appear to be dancing merrily off into the ocean. "I had to include that lighter blue," she says, "because I ran out of the other," and although she feels it is the dark indigo spiraling down from the top right that creates the movement in her quilt ("how I love the taste and texture of indigo"), it is the lightest of the three blues that catches the eye. Being willing to "make do" like this produces the refreshing spontaneity so evident in this charming piece. Takahashi began quiltmaking seven years ago but only started working with indigo fabrics after she joined the Kuroha Quilt Circle in 1983. This quilt was included in the circle's exhibition in New York in 1985 and was featured in the 1987 edition of *The Quilt Engagement Calendar.* Photograph courtesy the artist.

85. *Chattering of Cloths* by Ruri Miyamoto, Tokyo. 1985. 75″ x 75″ (190 x 190 cm). *Aizome* cottons and antique sarasa (Japanese batik). Hand-pieced and quilted. Here is another quilt by a talented member of Shizuko Kuroha's quilt circle. Miyamoto made this lively and wittily named piece for a group exhibition in which the basic quilt unit had either to be squares or triangles, so she chose a simple five-patch American pattern and gave it a distinctive Japanese look by an irregular placement of color. She named the quilt *Chattering of Cloths* because, she says, "I had all these lovely *aizome* cottons, and I chattered and chattered to them day after day as I worked out my design." She tells us that she had been collecting blue-and-white fabrics for years because the "warmth of old indigo seems to wrap around me," and like so many other Japanese quiltmakers she enjoys breathing new life into precious old fabrics. The center squares of her blocks are made from antique Japanese batik, while her lighter ones, "chattering merrily away to their companions," are old indigo cotton. It is said that indigo has seven shades that are achieved by repeated dippings in the dye bath. This quilt was exhibited in the Kuroha Quilt Circle exhibition in New York in 1985, and was featured in the 1987 edition of *The Quilt Engagement Calendar*. Photograph courtesy the artist.

86. *Aizome Baskets* by Harue Sato, Yokohama. 1984. 85″ x 85″ (215 x 215 cm). Old *aizome* fabrics. Hand-pieced, using the English method over papers, hand-quilted. This pattern, which appeared on a commemorative stamp in the U.S. in 1978, is Harue Sato's favorite, so she decided to use it to make this wonderful sampler of old Japanese *aizome* fabrics after she had found a collection of them in the family storehouse. In a country plagued by such hazards as earthquakes, typhoons, floods, and fires, the solidly built stone storehouse set apart from the family residence was an essential safeguard for family treasures. Sato's family were rice brokers in a country village, and so important members of their community. In Japan, up until the late nineteenth century, rice was the basic unit of currency (samurai, for example, received an annual stipend in the form of rice from their lord, which they then sold to the rice broker for cash). Sato's grandmother had many beautiful pieces of *aizome*, some of which were stencil-dyed for her at the local dye-shop on cloth she had woven herself. Having discovered this forgotten treasure, the quiltmaker was determined to give these old textiles a new lease on life by combining them into a beautiful design. She then *sashiko*-quilted her work and says, "It was hard going because the thread and the fabric were so thick."

87. *Flower Calendar* by Emi Yamamoto, Kyoto. 1985. Each block is 16″ x 16″ (42 x 42 cm). *Aizome* and solid cottons. Hand-pieced, appliquéd, and quilted. Flowers and flower-viewing ceremonies are closely tied to the cycles of Japanese life. In times past, farmers relied on flowering shrubs to tell them when to soak the seed rice to speed germination or when to till the paddies, and apart from the ubiquitous cherry blossom (the emblem of spring), other flowers are still associated with different months and seasons. When she found she had some small pieces of *aizome*, mostly stenciled with flower patterns, Yamamoto decided to make this charming flower calendar, but she made each block separate so that she could rotate and use them independently. She chose complementary quilting patterns whenever possible. January's "Pheasant Eye" is embellished with snowflakes. The Japanese grow their irises in water, so the block for May shows irises reflected in a stream. Morning Glory cannot grow without a support, so Yamamoto has placed this against a pattern derived from woven fencing. "As it always rains in June," she says, "I quilted slanting lines behind my hydrangea, a flower, incidentally, that is indigenous to Japan."

88. *Taketori Monogatari* ("The Tale of the Bamboo Cutter") by Emiko Toda Loeb, New York City. 1987.
72″ x 56″ (183 x 142 cm). Antique *aizome*, Indonesian batik, Japanese sarasa, and modern Japanese cottons.
The backing is made from old silk kimono. Machine-pieced, *sashiko*-quilted. Loeb explains that she wanted
to make a quilt that had the freedom of a Crazy quilt but without the overall patternless look of typical Crazy
design. This fascinating variation illustrates an old Japanese folktale of a couple who found a child in the
hollow of a piece of bamboo. She was, of course, a spirit, and when she grew up, having refused all the suitors
her adoptive parents found for her, she flew away to the moon. The strong verticals are intended to represent
the clean-cut lines of the tall and graceful bamboo, while the intersecting triangle of red and ochres on the left,
which animates the entire piece, is probably the "spirit" child. Loeb says both this quilt and *Hien* (see fig. 59)
represent a departure from her eleven previous quilts, which were more structured, such as *Denshoh*, the
magnificent Log Cabin variation illustrated in figures 23 and 23a. Unlike many of her fellow countrywomen
in Japan, Loeb is comfortable working with a sewing machine, although she always quilts by hand. "I used
sashiko here, but it was really hard on the fingers toward the end." As with her other distinctive quilts, Loeb
bought most of the fabrics from flea markets during her visits to Japan. *Taketori Monogatari* is illustrated in
the 1989 edition of *The Quilt Engagement Calendar*. Photograph courtesy the artist.

89. *Bamboo and Clouds* by Kazuko Yoshiura, Tokyo. 1987. 64″ x 47″ (163 x 120 cm). Indigo cotton, some old pieces of *kasuri*, *yukata*, and new cottons. Hand-appliquéd and *sashiko*-quilted. Yoshiura has worked her interesting quilt in the style of a Japanese screen painting, where cloud shapes rhythmically intersect and unite the painted areas (see fig. 46), although she tells us that she, in fact, took the idea from an antique kimono. She teaches *sashiko* professionally and was encouraged to try her hand at making a quilt by Miwako Kimura, whose *Sakura* is illustrated in figure 74, but she has not lost sight of the conventions of her craft. This lovely Japanese work is first and foremost a *sashiko* quilt. The clean vertical lines of the bamboo were worked on a single piece of cloth, and Yoshiura only padded the appliquéd sections: the little clamshells at the bottom and the familiar Japanese pattern at the upper left called *matsukawabishi* ("pine-bark diamond") because of its similarity to the patterning on the trunk of a pine tree. The quilt was then lined. "Most *sashiko* patterns are geometric grids," Yoshiura explains, "and I wanted to try and update this traditional stitching technique in some new way— update it and free it from the conformity of its past." In this delightfully fresh interpretation, the blank clouds offset her patterned areas in a true Japanese manner.

90. *Celebration* by Miyoko Kaga, Beppu City, Oita Prefecture. 1986. 90″ x 81″ (228 x 206 cm). *Aizome* cottons, antique *tsutsugaki*-dyed centerpiece. Hand-pieced, appliquéd, and quilted. This beautiful quilt celebrates the genius of Japanese dyers. In the center there is a magnificent example of *tsutsugaki*, a resist technique in which the design was drawn on the cloth freehand with a paper cone filled with rice paste, similar to frosting a cake. The quiltmaker found the center piece in an antiques shop and believes it was probably a *yutan*, a decorative covering for furniture. It is a felicitous design representing good fortune and long life, and in the past such designs were often dyed on cotton cloths that a bride took to her new home to cover the furniture and storage chests that came as part of her dowry. These lovely cloths played the same sort of role in a Japanese home as did a painting or a tapestry in Europe or the United States. When framing the center piece, Kaga tells us that she deliberately broke up the Wild Goose Chase border with irregular rectangles and minipatchwork blocks (look for Variable Star, Fan, and Bow Tie) because she dislikes too much continuity. The four corner crests are stylized plum blossoms that echo the realistic plum blossoms in the center. This unusual and typically Oriental quilt was exhibited at the International Quilt Festival in Houston, Texas, in 1987.

91. *The Waves* by Hiroko Nakamura, Toyohashi City, Aichi Prefecture. 1980. 79″ x 59″ (200 x 150 cm). Antique ramie. Hand-pieced and quilted. The fabrics Nakamura used for this appealing blue-and-white quilt were cut from an old samurai costume made for a festival in Kyoto more than a hundred years ago; the blue came from the distinctive wide-shouldered upper garment and the white from the kimono worn underneath. Because she wanted to explore the effects of counterchange, she chose an American pattern, Snail's Trail, which is similar to a pattern the Japanese used for small projects like bags and temple pouches about the same time that this samurai costume was made and which we saw in Iku Hara's quilt in figure 17. The fabric is ramie, the same bast-fiber cloth she used in her quilt in figure 92. "My patience was sorely tried," she says. "The fabric has a life of its own and runs away from the hands." She quilted the centers of the blue "waves" with motifs taken from Japanese heraldry (*kamon*). "Nobody had thought of *kamon* as quilting patterns in 1980, so none of my friends was at all encouraging!" However, the quilt turned out to be a winner, for it won her a prize in a local exhibition.

92. *Mariner's Compass* by Hiroko Nakamura, Toyohashi City, Aichi Prefecture. 1980. 69″ x 44″ (174 x 112 cm). Antique ramie and cotton *furoshiki*. Hand-pieced, hand-quilted, trapunto. Nakamura was using Japanese designs and fabrics in her quilts long before most other Japanese quiltmakers had thought of the idea. This classic Western-style nautical quilt is made from one of the bast-fiber fabrics (ramie) that rural Japan used for their clothing before the introduction of cotton in the eighteenth century. "I loved the blue and green coloring of the old kimono," Nakamura says. "It reminded me of the sea, but I did not enjoy working with it." Nakamura's quilting, as well as her piecing, is superb. Although the quilted motifs are Western in feeling, shells and anchors are featured among the Japanese designs, as befits an island nation like Japan. The circular echo-quilting surrounding the two Mariner's Compass blocks at the bottom reminds one of the raked gravel "waves" in a Zen garden.

93. *Morning Mist* by Kumiko Miura, Izumi City, Miyagi Prefecture. 1984. 71″ x 71″ (180 x 180 cm). *Aizu* cotton, American calicoes and cambrics. Hand-appliquéd and quilted. Her son kept pestering her to make him a blue-and-white quilt, so while she was planning this cool, restful piece, Kumiko Miura imagined herself walking through the woods in the early morning mist of summer. "I love the subtle stripes of so many of our traditional fabrics, so I visited our local textile mill and bought striped *aizu* cotton (used for everyday kimono) to mix with my other cottons to try and create the chevron effect of young leaves." Miura is a self-taught quiltmaker who was inspired by one of the exhibitions of antique American quilts that came to Japan in the early 1980s. She says "I create another self that is quite different from my usual domestic self. I am also very lucky because I have a husband who takes a great interest in my quilting and often helps me with my designing."

94. *Kasuri Quilt* by Shikae Wakafuji, Beppu City, Oita Prefecture. 1985. 71″ x 71″ (180 x 180 cm). *Kasuri* cotton and cream sheeting. *Sashiko*-quilted and assembled by hand. *Kasuri*, as we have already noted, is an imported weaving technique that wound its way from India, via Indonesia and Okinawa, to Japan. As is so often the case with a technique they import, the Japanese found a way of improving it, and in the nineteenth century they perfected a method of weaving pictures into the cloth. The technique involves stretching the undyed threads across a board and either drawing a freehand design on them in ink, or transferring an image with a stencil. The threads are then tied with hemp according to the marked design and dyed in the normal way. It is an intricate and time-consuming process, and for her elegant quilt Wakafuji chose a classic "picture *kasuri*" of a carp leaping out of the water, which she combined with blocks of a more conventional geometric *kasuri* pattern. To complement these two traditional designs, she *sashiko*-quilted the alternative blocks with a folding fan. Kyushu, where Wakafuji lives, is the center of *kasuri* production, and she tells us that she likes to keep these old handwoven fabrics as intact as possible, when making her quilts, as a tribute to the weaver's skill.

95. *The Coming of Halley's Comet* by Chizuko Tatsuyama, Beppu City, Oita Prefecture. 1985. 68″ x 68″ (172 x 172 cm). Old *aizome* prints, *kasuri*, and striped woven cottons, Japanese sheeting. Hand-pieced and quilted. This quiltmaker is interested in combining Japanese indigo-dyed fabrics with American patterns because she believes it changes their character and gives them new life. "I originally planned a sampler quilt, but while I was working I found I liked star patterns and Mariner's Compass, so after seeing a quilt I admired in *Quilter's Newsletter Magazine* I changed my mind and made a Medallion to commemorate the coming of Halley's comet instead." Mothers of schoolchilden in Japan collect rags and used paper to be recycled to raise money for school projects, and Tatsuyama gleaned some of her fabrics from this source, including a pair of children's pajamas made from Okinawan *kasuri*, which she used as the dark accent in the corner blocks. Because some of these old fabrics were "tired," the quilter backed them with Pellon, and enlivened them still further by introducing kimono silks in her center blocks. She took up quiltmaking in 1981 and loves the craft for the eloquent way it unites the past with the present. "I am also keen that my children should understand the value and importance of slow rhythmic stitching in this 'instant' jet age!"

96. *Ripples of Water* by Koishi Okabe, Oita City, Oita Prefecture. 1985. 79″ x 79″ (200 x 200 cm). *Kasuri* and white cotton sheeting. Hand-pieced and quilted. This refreshing quilt, reminiscent of white foam-topped waves on a windy day, was made by a quilter who enjoys marrying traditional American patterns with Japanese fabrics. "My mother gave me an old *kasuri futon* cover, and because Winding Ways is my favorite pattern I decided to use both and see what happened. I was pleased with the way it turned out, because my children like modern designs," Okabe says. The *kasuri*, with its unique "splashed" patterns achieved in the dyeing process and framed here by a border of crisp navy and white checks, has a striking contemporaneity that the maker has enhanced with a fine stylized quilting pattern.

97. *Bishamon Kikko* by Masako Kawada, Tokushima City, Tokushima Prefecture. 1985. 87″ x 71″ (220 x 180 cm). Cotton crepes and indigo-dyed cottons. Hand-pieced and hand-quilted. The maker of this fresh country-style quilt took the pattern from her mother's bridal obi. "It's usually considered to be a masculine pattern," Kawada explains, "because you find it on samurai armor, swords, or men's kimono. Although I made the quilt in memory of my mother, I am giving it to my son, so I thought the pattern doubly appropriate." Her mother's bridal obi may well have been made of a much richer material than Kawada has used here, but she chose not to work with precious silks ("it's the ordinary Japanese fabrics that speak loudest to me"), so she bought cotton crepes normally used for everyday kimono from her local textile factory. The blues are all indigo-dyed cottons. "Indigo is beautiful when it is new, but it is even more beautiful as it ages. There are supposed to be seven different shades and I wanted to explore them all," Kawada says, although this has not prevented her from introducing other colors, such as a single flash of yellow to catch the eye. She says making quilts is a form of meditation for her. "While I stitch, I pray for the safety of my son and husband, and when my quilts are finished they become my legacy." Kawada is the wife of a doctor and is entirely self-taught.

98. *Dusk* by Yoshimi Morinaga, Kamimashiki Gun, Kumamoto Prefecture. 1985. 79″ x 64″ (200 x 163 cm). Cotton *kasuri*, solid indigo, denim, and cotton prints. Hand-pieced, appliquéd, and quilted. The maker of this superb scene of birds flying across the ocean in the evening light has given a Japanese twist to the old American pattern, Drunkard's Path, combining it with striped fabric to create the distinctive curly-topped waves so often seen in Japanese woodblock prints. "My mother-in-law gave me an old *kasuri* kimono that my father-in-law had worn as a teenager, so I planned to make a quilt for them both," Morinaga explains. "But they didn't know what a quilt was, so I made a quilted summer *futon* cover instead." Because much of her fabric was unseasonably dark, Morinaga bleached indigo cotton to create a contrast of subtly graded blues. She says she is not particularly interested in creating designs that are specifically Japanese (although this quilt is unmistakably Japanese in color and feeling), but she is interested in working with fabrics that "have lived longer than I have." She took up quiltmaking in 1979, and her work has won several awards. "I find it so creative," the artist says, "even though it is difficult to translate my imaginary designs into a quilted reality." This lovely composition is a testimony to her skill.

99. *Nebula* by Ginko Ito, Kushiro City, Hokkaido. 1985. 83″ x 80″ (210 x 204 cm). Old cotton *aizome* prints. Hand-pieced and quilted. The dictionary definition of "nebula" is a cloud of distant stars, and in this intricately pieced quilt, Ito has captured a twinkling night sky to perfection. She says she had no particular design concept in mind before she started, but because she enjoys improvising and abstract painting, and was working with so many midnight blue fabrics contrasted with white, the scheme just fell into place. The pleasurable part was spreading the fabrics around the house and developing subtle shifts of color to create the vortex in the center. The hard part was cutting the patches, not because of the tedium (which would have been understandable), but because of the natural reverence the Japanese have for their old textiles. "I felt so sorry for them because I had to cut them up," she says. Itō is a member of the Kuroha Quilt Circle and admits that her *sensei's* ("teacher's") influence on her has been enormous. This quilt was hung in the group exhibition in New York in 1985 and appeared the same year at the "Quilt in Japan" exhibition at Laforet Museum in Tokyo.

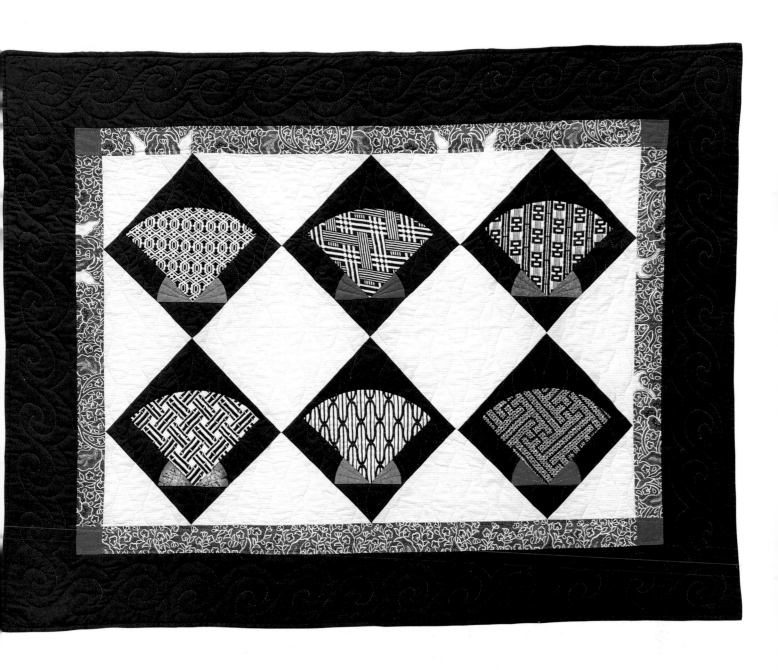

100. *The Quilt of Many Credits* by Yuko Watanabe, Tokyo. 1987. 55″ x 42″ (140 x 106 cm). *Yukata* cottons, Indonesian batik, dress cottons. Hand-pieced by Watanabe, quilted by Teruko Nakayama. "Having been a critic of other people's quilts for nearly four years in my role as editor of *Patchwork Quilt Tsūshin*, I felt it was time I tried my hand at this creative process," says Yuko Watanabe. "So I picked an easy seashell pattern and set to work to make a wall hanging for our new apartment. I feel that planning a quilt is like planning a vacation: it should be organized but should have some freedom left too." This led her to piece together each block from samples of *yukata* cotton without worrying too much about the overall balance of tone and pattern, but the result works together wonderfully well. *(Note from her British coauthor*: Only a Japanese would have put in that flick of red in the bottom right block!) "As usual, I owe everything to my friends," Yuko continues. "The fabrics came from an indigo-dyeing factory owned by some friends; Junko Misawa, who works with me on the magazine, acted as adviser and sewed the blocks together for me; I chose quilting patterns related to water, and Jill provided the templates; and Teruko quilted it for me beautifully in just ten days. Hence the title: *The Quilt of Many Credits*. Then, because my husband, Wanchai, so enjoyed watching me sew in the evenings instead of working, I dedicated it to him: 'A Japanese quilt from your not very typical Japanese wife!' Photograph courtesy Kazuo Saito.

101. *Tsutomu's Quilt* by Michiko Kondo, Ako City, Hyogo Prefecture. 1986. 66″ x 48″ (168 x 122 cm). Cottons. Hand-appliquéd, reverse-appliqué. A photograph just can't do justice to the staggering complexity of this quilt that Michiko Kondo made from a snapshot of her son. Fascinated by newspaper photographs, which are composed of halftone dots, Kondo had a professional separation made that she then enlarged to actual size on a photocopier, and from this made her pattern. "It took me two months to figure out how even to start working," she tells us, "and another four months to finish the quilt!" She first traced her son's image on the background fabric and divided it into a 1¼″ (3 cm) grid. She basted blue fabric underneath the white, and worked the boy's hair and features in reverse-appliqué, maintaining the basic grid. The remaining 600-odd dots at each intersection of the grid are appliquéd. This is Kondo's first original design; she had always worked before with American patterns and usually in pastel colors. "I started to make quilts five years ago when we moved to a village in Nagano Prefecture, and there was nothing to do, so I took classes," she says. "I find that quiltmaking is a wonderful way of expressing myself, and as I finish each quilt, I feel that I have been enriched by the process."

Country Textiles

In the last fifty years or so, Japan has become one of the most urban countries in the world, but as a corollary to this urbanism there is often a feeling of nostalgia. In the grind of huge cities today, we all look over our shoulders to a past where the bad things have been forgotten and the good are enshrined in the glowing sepia tones of an old photograph—a mistiness that brings to mind the *kasuri* cottons we discussed in the previous chapter. Nostalgia among Japanese quilters is expressed by the use of the humble fabrics of village life to construct quilts with the rough feel and smoky coloring of rusticity. We have made a special section to display some of these country-inspired quilts.

Nostalgia is an interesting phenomenon. In the West, there also seems to be a longing for the light of oil lamps, the smell of raw oats, and the feel of binder twine: strange to those of us who lived with all of these things and now rejoice in electricity, breakfast cereals, and Scotch-tape. In Japan, however, the nostalgia is closer to home. Vast city although it is, Tokyo is essentially still a collection of many villages, and a detour from a main thoroughfare will soon bring you

into a world of "mom-and-pop" shops, village stores, market stalls, and flimsy wooden buildings. Fabrics that seemed sentenced to death by the introduction of synthetics have survived because the government actively promotes these rural crafts even if the cloth itself is now woven in the middle of an urban sprawl.

Apart from the indigo-dyed *aizome* and *kasuri*-woven cottons, quilters have used materials with romantic-sounding names whose origins lie deep in Japan's past. *Jofu* and ramie are woven from the fibers of a nettle plant, and *tsumugi* is a type of raw silk made from damaged cocoons that have been rejected by the silk spinners. There are also more mundane fabrics such as those cut from *futon* covers, *furoshiki*, country-style kimono cottons, woolens, knits, and corduroys.

The design themes are eclectic in this section,

102. White *sashiko*-stitching on indigo-dyed cotton is now one of the favorite Japanese hobbies. Photograph courtesy Yuko Watanabe.

echoing other sections of our book. There are quilts that use *kamon* (patterns taken from the Japanese heraldic crests), hybrid quilts using traditional American themes, and blue-and-white quilts. There are also abstract quilts, but the majority are pictorial, representing country scenery or society. One ingenious quiltmaker even uses the craft to record social history!

Rural stitchery is a natural feature; *sashiko*, which was once used for binding layers of fabric together, here creates complex patterns to highlight the indigo background of a quilt.

As you will see from one of the quilts in this section,

the Japanese government gives craftsmen and craftswomen, whose ancient and special skills are in danger of becoming extinct, an award that carries with it an annual stipend and the title "Living National Treasure," with the understanding that they will train apprentices and so keep their skills alive for future generations. This award is not just limited to crafts, for the performing arts are also honored in this way, but textile production and such allied crafts as dyeing and stencil-cutting are prominently supported. Thus, in this case, the way back seems to be the way forward.

103a. 1982. 39″ x 25″ (100 x 63 cm). An elderly woman carrying heavy bags in a street in Okamoto's hometown, Nagoya. Note the *kasuri*-dyed kimono and the two bags: one is traditional indigo-dyed cotton and the other is modern plastic. Japanese country women used to pull their hair into a tight bun at the back of their heads, which then caused the hairline to recede.

103b. 1981. 39″ x 27″ (100 x 69 cm). A traditional striped coat is worn here over an apron and kimono. The woman carries her shopping tied up in a *furoshiki*, with more wrapped in a cloth and slung from her shoulders.

103c. 1982. 39″ x 26″ (100 x 65 cm). Country people glean firewood from the thinnings of forest trees, and this quilt shows an old woman carrying the traditional pronged stick with which they pull down the branches. She is without shoes because her extra-thick work-socks have special rubber soles. Okamoto brushed the logo on the traditional indigo apron with bleach, and quilted the background to show a typical Japanese dry-stone wall.

103a–103e. *Women of Traditional Japan* by Yasuko Okamoto, Nagoya City, Aichi Prefecture. 1981–1983. Old *kasuri*, striped cotton, hand-dyed cottons, woolens, cords, plastic, wool. Hand-appliquéd, crocheted, embroidered, and quilted. Although the maker of this remarkable series of quilts prefers to be considered a social anthropologist, her fine eye for detail and her superb craftsmanship prove that she is also an outstanding artist. In the early seventies, Okamoto formed a group to research and document Japanese folk traditions before they completely disappeared. Initially, the work was carried out in a village near her home, each member of the group choosing a different subject: for example, rural architecture, crops, agricultural tools and methods. Because she had trained as a fashion designer, Okamoto decided she would concentrate on clothing. "I found that the villagers were reserved, like country people everywhere, but women are always prepared to talk about their clothes. Although I started off by making detailed drawings, I soon decided that I wanted a true record of the shapes of the clothes and of the lovely old country fabrics, so I switched to appliqué quilts

103d. 41″ x 31″ (104 x 78 cm). An island woman carries a stock of vegetables away from her terraced garden in the hills. She wears *monpe*, the traditional baggy trousers of the working population, but hers are made of modern fabric. This and her patterned pinafore identify her as being relatively young.

103e. 1981. 39″ x 21″ (100 x 54 cm). Okamoto crocheted the vest this woman wears and braided the straps of her basket from rags. Here the *monpe* are made of *kasuri*, which is the normal fabric used for these trousers. The quilted fir trees in the background indicate a mountain environment.

instead as a method of recording my research." The result of this particular study was called "The Disappearing Village." Okamoto later turned her attention to people and clothing in other regions, and as a result she has made a unique record of the traditional life of Japan: a superb quilted documentary that is a visual feast for the eye. "I try to get to know my subjects if I can," she says, "and use pieces of their own clothing where possible. Or I buy the kind of blouses, skirts, aprons, and scarves that they wear from the local stores and cut these up. Everything in my quilts is historically accurate." As you will see, her warmth and humor, her fine eye for detail, and her artistry has made these quilts more than just a memorial. The figures live: the clothes wrinkle and sag just as clothes do in reality; her exquisite embroidery catches fleeting expressions, while the realistic quilted details in the backgrounds of each piece place the women in their correct environments. The quilts are masterpieces, and this unique social documentary has been acclaimed everywhere it has been exhibited in Japan. Photographs courtesy Susumu Tomita.

104. *Country Shoes* by Yasuko Okamoto, Nagoya City, Aichi Prefecture. 1980. 70″ x 67″ (179 x 171 cm). Solid and printed cottons, woolens, knits, corduroy, plastic. Hand-appliquéd, embroidered, and quilted. While making her brilliant quilted portrayals of rural Japanese life, Okamoto also decided to record shoes for posterity—not necessarily traditional shoes, she explains, but the variety that you see on the streets today. The focus of her study was a market held each month at her local Buddhist temple, and in this original and highly entertaining quilt Okamoto's sensitive eye has caught the stance of a group of middle-aged shoppers. Here are busy women in search of a bargain; determined women; hesitant women; elderly women whose feet hurt; others who are exhausted—and one who has had enough and is pushing off for home! Many shoes sold in Japan today are cheap plastic models that you can pick up in the supermarket, and Okamoto has recorded these also. She used genuine stocking material and worked it so that it wrinkled just as it tends to do on elderly legs. This remarkable artist has also made a similar record of women's handbags as a companion to this perceptive study. Photograph courtesy Susumu Tomita.

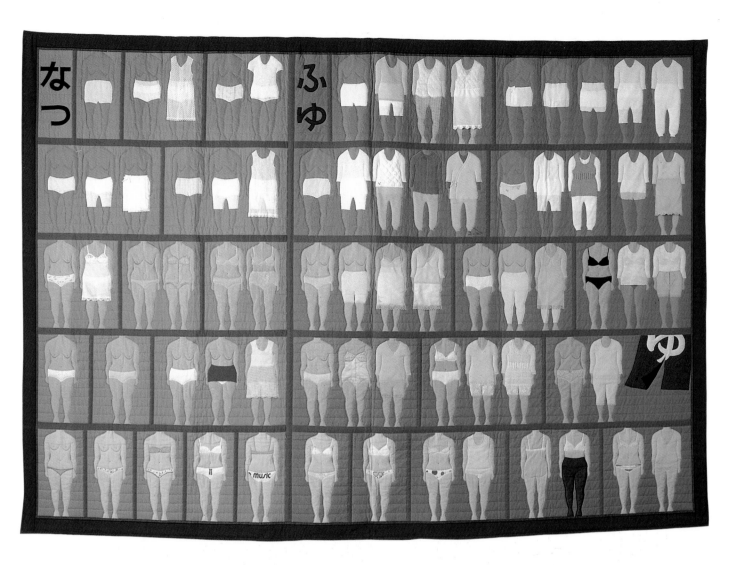

105. *Japanese Underwear* by Yasuko Okamoto, Nagoya City, Aichi Prefecture. 1983. 76″ x 109″ (192 x 278 cm).
Silks, cottons, knits, sateens, lace, elastic, and elasticized cotton. Hand-appliquéd, embroidered, and quilted.
In this witty piece, Okamoto affectionately illustrates the diverse underwear of three generations of Japanese
women. She tells us that she took a year to do the research by visiting her local public bath and watching
country women peel off their layers of clothing before submerging themselves in the steaming water. Each
framed panel represents the underwear of one woman. The top two rows show the underclothing of elderly
women. The next two rows are devoted to middle-aged women; and the bottom row, with its bikini briefs and
black tights, belongs to the young. Okamoto divided the quilt into summer and winter seasons: summer, on the
left, has the mauve background; winter, on the right, has the gray. So we are privileged to see here the
underpinnings of a nation: the briefs, the bloomers, the corselets, the quilted vests, the knitted stomachers, the
lace-edge slips, and the long johns. This must be the only quilt in the world to have captured a nation almost
in the raw—a percipient social study and a fascinating one! Photograph courtesy Susumu Tomita.

106. *The Old Homes* by Kanoko Takeuchi, Oita City, Oita Prefecture. 1986. 56″ x 45″ (143 x 115 cm). Old *aizome, kasuri*, cotton sheeting, cotton prints. Reverse-appliqué, appliqué, and quilting. Takeuchi wanted to find a way of expressing the soul of Japan, so she chose to illustrate four traditional Japanese buildings in this picturesque and architecturally revealing quilt; the idea came from a modern woodblock print. At top left there is a traditional farmhouse with its steep-pitched thatched roof; top right is the granite-walled keep of a castle in her locality; bottom right, a shed where a farmer might keep his tools backed by the silhouette of a farmhouse showing the traditional jutting roof-beam; and bottom left, the Japanese family storehouse. Both rural and urban families used to keep their valuables in solid stone buildings set apart from the wooden family dwelling as a protection against fire and earthquakes, and at one time these attractive, white-plastered buildings could be seen all over Japan. "I design as I sew," Takeuchi tells us, "and I found creating my own world in each of these four pictures very satisfying." Takeuchi is self-taught, but now belongs to a group. She has participated in four group exhibitions.

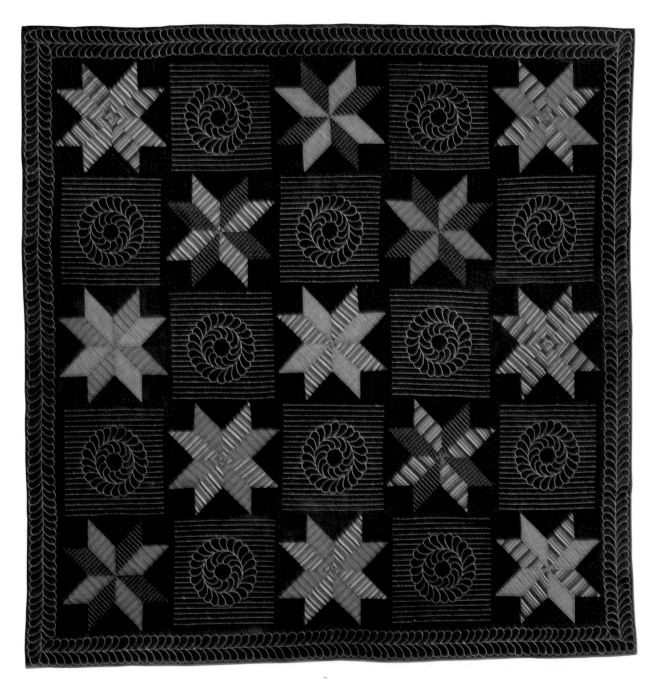

107. *Windmills* by Sawako Tsurugiji, Kanazawa City, Ishikawa Prefecture. 1978. 71″ x 71″ (180 x 180 cm).
Striped kimono cottons and indigo-dyed cotton. Hand-pieced, *sashiko*-quilted. "I live in northwest Japan,"
says this quiltmaker, "where the winters are long and cold, so I needed to make something practical and
decided to make a *kotatsu* ("heater") cover that all the family could enjoy." (The Mino family can be seen
enjoying the warmth of a *kotatsu* quilt in the top photograph on page 110.) She tells us that the striped
"windmills" are pieced from the old work clothing of her father, who died while she was making the quilt. "I
was so glad I used his fabric in my blocks; it gives us all a happy memory of him." She set her colorful blocks
together with squares of indigo-dyed cotton evenly quilted with white *sashiko* cotton. "It was tough pulling the
rough yarn through the thick indigo, so I had to do it by the laborious 'up-and-down method.'" But her patience
was rewarded: every stitch is perfect. Her family says that this quilt was made during her "Blue Period," for
she has now moved on to working with kimono silks, and one of her new silk quilts is illustrated in figure 62.

107a. Even modern Japanese houses don't have much central heating, so families keep themselves warm on a winter's evening by tucking themselves up in a quilt spread over a special table with a heater called a *kotatsu*, which is attached to the underside. Here you can see the Mino family enjoying an evening tucked up snugly in their family-made patchwork *kotatsu* quilt. Father Tetsuji Mino cut and marked the patches; Mother Kimiko sewed them together; and their two daughters, Momoko, age four, and Fuko, age two, stuffed the squares. Photograph courtesy Reiko Ariyoshi.

107b. In a traditional Japanese home, where bedding is stored away in closets during the day, *kotatsu* covers are one way in which American quiltmaking techniques can be put to good use. Here is a striking patchwork *kotatsu* quilt made by Hiroko Fukumoto of Tokushima City, Tokushima Prefecture, with both new and old indigo-dyed cottons. The quilt name is *Puss in the Corner*; it was made in 1985; and the dimensions of the piece are 75″ x 75″ (190 x 190 cm).

108. *In Praise of Tsumugi* by Tomiko Kikuchi, Toride City, Ibaragi Prefecture. 1980. 83″ x 46″ (210 x 117 cm). *Tsumugi* ("raw silk"). Hand-pieced and quilted. The maker of this lively quilt was born in an area where the local fabric *tsumugi* is famous, so she decided to commemorate its vivid coloring in a quilt. This country-style fabric, with its natural slubbed texture and its capacity to mold itself comfortably to the body, is a popular fabric for everyday kimono. It was made originally from split or damaged cocoons by farmers' wives for family use, and as it could not be reeled off, it had to be carded and spun. During the spinning process, the country women moistened the silk filaments with their saliva, and tradition would have it that the best *tsumugi* was made by middle-aged women because the saliva of young women contained too many hormones, which damaged the silk. Also, beautiful women are supposed to have made better *tsumugi* than plain ones! Kikuchi worked her quilt in many colors, framing the central design with an interesting strip-pieced border of triangles. She certainly is one of Japan's more fortunate quilters, for in a country where living space is at a premium, her husband has built her a two-story studio in their yard. "I quilt there for ten hours a day sometimes," she tells us.

109. *Choryu* ("Tide" or "Current") by Kayoko Oguri, Kaifu Gun, Tokushima Prefecture. 1983. 79″ x 63″ (200 x 160 cm). *Shijira* cottons (a type of crisp crepe used for summer kimono) and indigo-dyed cottons. Hand-pieced and quilted. This quiltmaker has made a specialty of designing with squares and triangles, and in this asymmetrical composition she has used these geometric shapes to create a dramatically kinetic quilt. "I live in a part of Japan where the sea runs through a narrow channel between two islands, and when it meets the incoming tide, it swirls into massive whirlpools," she explains. "I tried to reproduce this flowing, swirling water in fabric." She bought most of her cottons from local textile firms and says that because so few women now wear kimono, the demand for the attractively textured *shijira* crepe has fallen off, and she hopes by using it for quilts, she will stimulate a new interest in it. "Quiltmaking has become an important medium of expression for the ordinary housewives of Japan, but I am intrigued by the way this once purely domestic craft is now being appreciated as art. Our quilts will live on long after we have gone," she says. One of Oguri's quilts won an award in a local art exhibition, and another made by her group received second Grand Prix at the Tokushima Art Festival.

110. *Monpe Quilt* by Keiko Goke, Sendai City, Miyagi Prefecture. 1985. 83″ x 69″ (210 x 175 cm). Old *aizome* cottons, silks, and solid cottons. Machine-pieced, hand-quilted. Behind this vivid contemporary quilt lies a touching story that illustrates the deep affection the Japanese feel for their old traditional textiles. Goke trained as a graphic designer and worked in Tokyo until she married and settled down in her hometown, Sendai, in northwestern Japan. She tells us that she wanted to make a quilt inspired by her rural environment, and by chance met an elderly woman dyer (fig. 110a), whose mother had been awarded by the Japanese government the title of "Living National Treasure" to commemorate a lifetime of working with textiles, cultivating hemp, dyeing, spinning, and weaving. "She was about to burn a pile of fabrics that included a whole kimono and fragments of *monpe* [the baggy trousers seen in figs. 103d and 103e], which had been dyed by her famous mother. I managed to save some of the fabrics and decided to work them into a quilt in memory of this wonderful old lady. I didn't want to use a traditional Japanese design, but decided to renew the cloth by arranging it in a contemporary design. Quiltmaking is like painting for me. I sketch a basic idea, but then improvise as I go along. I had to quilt closely because some of the old fabrics were really tired." With some trepidation Goke showed the contemporary quilt to her elderly friend and was delighted by her reaction. "She felt her mother's work had been given a second life," Goke says. "I believe those old fabrics had been waiting for me, and it was my honor to restore the work of one of our Living National Treasures."

110a. Keiko Goke met Yoshino Chiba, the daughter of a famous Japanese dyer who was made a "Living National Treasure" during her lifetime and some of whose fabrics she incorporated in her quilt. Yoshino Chiba is seen here with the indigo plants she cultivates. She has followed in her mother's footsteps and is also a dyer.

111. *Kagome* by Keiko Yamaguchi, Tokyo. 1986. 93″ x 81″ (235 x 205 cm). Cotton and *tsumugi* (a country-style silk fabric with a slubbed texture). Hand-pieced and hand-quilted. Yamaguchi's intention was to create a basketweave pattern (*kagome* means "basketweave") in order to evoke the feeling of the seaside: "a fisherman's basket left on the beach," she says. Her pattern is, in fact, a hexagon, but in putting it together Yamaguchi changed the color sequences so that it emerged as an intricate triangular design. "I felt that the uneven edges created by the construction looked like a shoreline, with the sea breaking over the golden sand," she explains. "The basket in the center looks a little lonely, but there is happiness there; perhaps the fisherman left it on the beach while he went off to sell his catch." She has completed her sea theme by quilting the golden "sand" with two patterns related to water: "blue waves" (*seigaiha*) on the left and "fishing net" (*ami*) on the right. Yamaguchi says that her designing skills are influenced by her many hobbies. "I am a great knitter, and I hand-knit ten to twenty sweaters every season. I enjoy macramé, Japanese and French embroidery, woodcarving, and also other crafts like pottery."

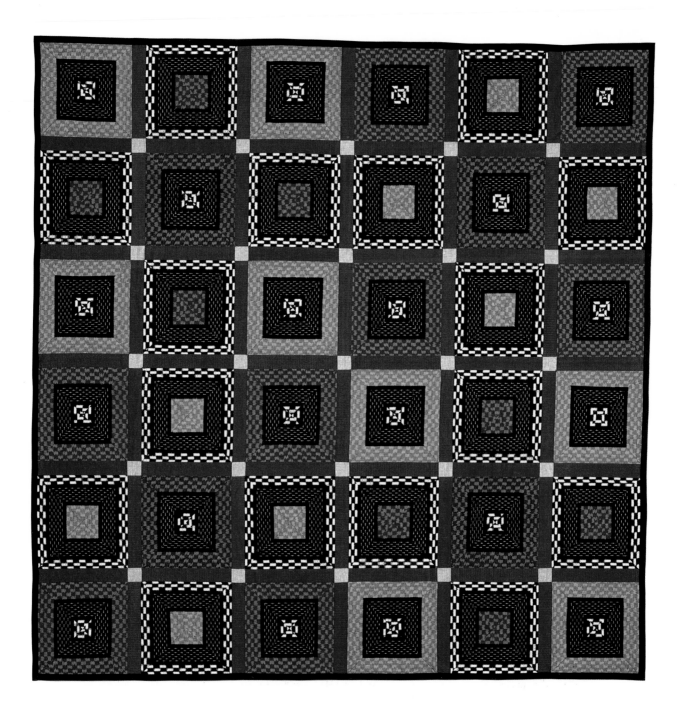

112. *Kasuri Collection* by Mayumi Tanaka, Mizuma Gun, Fukuoka Prefecture. 1983. 87″ x 79″ (220 x 200 cm). *Kasuri* cotton and solid indigo cottons. Hand-pieced and tied. The maker of this strong, dignified quilt comes from a family of *kasuri* weavers and lives in a part of Japan famed for this warm splash-patterned fabric. All the fabrics that Tanaka has used in her quilt are new. She bought them from local textile factories, or they came from her own family textile business. She pieced them in the popular pattern called *mimasu*, meaning "nested measuring boxes," which is also a Japanese heraldic emblem. This is very much a local quilt, so it is only fitting that it should have won "Best of Show" in a major exhibition of handicrafts made from the *kasuri* of her region. Other quilts of Tanaka's using this lovely resist-dyed fabric have also won her prizes. "I want to try and publicize the beauty of *kasuri* cottons, particularly those made in my own hometown," she tells us.

113. *The Castle Quilt* by Miyoko Yano, Kasugai City, Aichi Prefecture. 1986. 48″ x 40″ (123 x 102 cm). Old *futon* and kimono fabrics, old indigo-dyed cottons, and hand-dyed modern fabrics. Hand-pieced and appliquéd. When she was a child, Miyoko Yano used to attend festivals in the grounds of the local castle, joyous happy occasions, she says, which she wanted to commemorate in a quilt. As well as creating pictures of birds, flowers, or majestic carp (see fig. 94), weavers of Japanese *kasuri* also depicted architecture such as a famous late-nineteenth-century woven castle similar to the one in this quilt. "It always reminds me of our local castle," Yano explains, "and because it was a geometric pattern it was easy to reproduce in patchwork. I chose my colors to reflect the evening sky, my favorite time of day, and as I worked I checked my coloring against the sunsets I could see from my window." Yano makes and wears her own kimono, so she had plenty of leftover scraps that she combined with printed fabric from an old *futon* cover. "In order to maintain the same palette, I had to dye some extra pieces myself, using vegetable dyes extracted from camellia, grenadine, tea, and other flowers." Yano is a nurse, but like so many other women in these caring professions, she finds quiltmaking therapeutic. "I create my memories and my dreams in my quilts," she says. "And I can also restore life to the old country fabrics I love so much."

114. *Images of Autumn* by Naoko Izumisawa, Ashigarakami Gun, Kanagawa Prefecture. 1985. 55″ x 43″ (140 x 110 cm). Old *kasuri* cottons, solid and hand-bleached cottons, Velcro. Hand-pieced, appliquéd, and quilted. The working clothes of country people are often made of *kasuri* cotton, particularly baggy trousers called *monpe*. Izumisawa's mother gave her an old pair of *monpe* that she cut up and combined with aniline-dyed cotton in this charming rustic wall hanging—a striking combination of old and new. The design was inspired by one of her own flower arrangements, and she went to immense pains to achieve the right textures: the seedheads are fashioned from strips of dyed Velcro, and she frayed hand-bleached cotton to create pampas flowers. "My husband got sick while I was making this quilt," Izumisawa reminisces, "and as I waited at the hospital while he underwent surgery, I sat fraying bits of cotton to make these flowers; I must have made more than a hundred of them!" They will doubtless find their way into another quilt for Izumisawa is a quilt addict (her remarkable *Kirigami* is illustrated in fig. 47). The cutoff corner at the lower right is a typical Japanese stratagem to challenge the eye by breaking the regularity of the center medallion.

115. *Bellflowers* by Toyoko Fujisaki, Sapporo City, Hokkaido. 1986. 77″ x 75″ (196 x 190 cm). Kimono silks and *jofu* (a finely woven fabric made from plant fibers). Hand-pieced, quilted, and embroidered. Here is a quilt that clearly illustrates the lovely Japanese resist-dyed patterns and also shows the skillful way quiltmakers use them to their best advantage. Before cotton cultivation became established in the eighteenth century, bast-fiber fabrics were the only alternative to silk. Country people used them for work clothing, but finer varieties were also woven for the ruling classes and rich city merchants. Fujisaki was given this piece, elegantly patterned with bellflowers (one of the traditional "Seven Plants of Autumn"), and wanting to keep as much of it as intact as possible, she combined it with panels of four-patch blocks that were made from her own bridal kimono and others given to her by family and friends. "I wanted my quilt to be a homage to the kimono," Fujisaki explains. "Making a kimono is an important occasion in a woman's life." Fujisaki often dyes cotton for her other quilts with dyes she extracts herself from home-grown plants. "By planting the seeds in the spring, harvesting them in the autumn, and making quilts during the bitterly cold days of winter, I feel I am part of nature's cycle." This lovely and uniquely Japanese piece is quilted all over with a design of spritely plovers, further illustrating Fujisaki's empathy with the natural world.

116. *Furoshiki Mola Quilt* by Keiko Minato, Hiroshima. 1985. 32″ x 33″ (82 x 84 cm). Cotton *furoshiki*, Japanese sheeting, coarse netting. Reverse-appliqué and embroidery. After seeing an exhibition of molas, Keiko Minato was inspired to try the art herself. "I didn't feel capable of making the geniune thing, so I adapted the technique by using a printed *furoshiki* and inserting colored sheeting under the surface to give the illusion of layers," she explains. She also created interesting textural effects by adding coarse netting and embroidering some flowers and leaves and outlining the scrolling vines. She feels that her unique "Oriental" mola somehow looks more Chinese than Japanese, as red peonies and scrolling vines is a typical Chinese design. However, the soft pinks in some of the flower petals and the vivid flashes of purple and orange betray its Japanese provenance. Minato also made the pretty basketweave crib quilt seen in figure 61. "All my quilts are made from old clothing or from bits and pieces given to me by friends and family," she says.

Kamon Quilts

A wonderful source of quilt patterns resides in Japanese heraldry: the *kamon* of this section's title. Ironically, it was a source first largely exploited by foreign quiltmakers, both in Japan and in the United States, but the Japanese have swiftly followed foreign example and are now making full use of the marvelous decorative motifs found in their heraldic handbooks.

A famous Japanese scholar once defined good pattern as the "portrayal of essence," and the anonymous craftsmen who designed these heraldic insignia have certainly succeeded in capturing the very essence of Japan. These lively pictorial images vividly illustrate the identification the Japanese have with nature, together with the value placed on the ordinary tools of existence, and they include most of the significant and religious motifs common to Japanese life (fig. 1).

Kamon means "family crest," but the characters used

117. 11 typical *kamon* designs.

118. The Japanese invented the folding fan, and it is a symbol of both masculine authority and feminine elegance. This black military fan was probably just ceremonial, and the crest is based on the heart-shaped leaves of wood sorrel, but with sword blades inserted between each leaf. Edo period (1600–1867). Photograph courtesy the Trustees of the British Museum, London.

to write the word can also be read as "family-textile-figure," for the earliest crests were taken from the figured patterns in the woven silks and brocades worn at the imperial court in Kyoto in the eleventh century. This luxury-loving aristocratic society sought a method for personal identification, so they began extracting a motif from the designs of their favorite textiles and then had these painted on their personal possessions, including the canopies of their ox-drawn carriages.

Although the first "carriage crests," as they were called, owed their existence to textiles, decorative inspiration soon broadened to include numerous designs from nature so dear to the Japanese heart: flowers, grasses, birds, and insects. And when the country was plunged into civil war, thus making battle heraldry necessary to identify combatants, these courtly emblems influenced the heraldic style. A military fan decorated with a crest based on the leaves of wood sorrel, a shy wild flower, is illustrated in figure 118. Fans are a masculine accessory in Japan.

Aristocratic rank and heraldry were officially abolished after World War II, but *kamon* continue to play an important part in Japanese life. Families cling to their family crest, and the degree of formality of a kimono, for example, is determined by the number of crests dyed across the shoulders: five for a ceremonial robe; three for less formal wear. Shops, airlines, municipalities, and restaurants have borrowed from this heraldic source for their logos, and you also find these delightful motifs printed on cotton textiles, shopping bags, and even wrapping paper because they are valued now for their purely decorative appeal.

There is an element of purity about *kamon* designs

that lends itself particularly well to the quilting medium. The motifs are refined to their essentials so that the object portrayed is reduced to the simplest linear expression: ideal for patchwork, appliqué, or as quilting patterns. Nor do they have to be used as they appear in the official handbooks; individual elements can be extracted and reworked in many ways. They are a lexicon of Japanese design for everybody.

Many types of fabric have been used to make *kamon* quilts, one of the most popular being the fresh blue-and-white *yukata* cottons, the fabric that is used for the Japanese summer kimono. The *yukata* was originally a simple bathrobe made of some kind of bast-fiber material, but it acquired fashionable notoriety in the early nineteenth century. The military government, infuriated as usual by the excesses of the merchant classes, banned them from wearing certain kinds of fabric and "upper-class" colors. Cotton was becoming fashionable then, and although their daily garb was suitably subdued to pass muster, city folk satisfied their yearning for ornate patterns by having them stencil-dyed on their bathrobes and then wore these out in the streets during hot evenings. The *yukata* has been an indispensable part of the Japanese summer scene ever since. Sueko Murata models a *yukata* for us in figure 119, and the first of the foreign-made *kamon*-and-*yukata* quilts that started a fashion among quiltmakers in Tokyo is shown in figure 120.

Foreign-made quilts based on Japanese designs are becoming increasingly popular. Now that we have reached the final section of our book, we hope that it will encourage a flow of new ideas between quilt-makers everywhere.[9]

119. The pretty blue-and-white cotton summer kimono called *yukata* is seldom seen in the streets of Japan today, but nearly everybody wears one at home. Here Sueko Murata is smartly dressed in a *yukata* decorated with rippling water and sashed with an obi of red linen. She wears on her feet the traditional *geta*, which are thonged wooden sandals. She carries the round summer fan that has also become a heraldic emblem, and she has used this pattern in her quilt illustrated in figure 123. Photograph courtesy Kazuo Saito.

120. *The Granddaddy of Them All*. A group quilt made by Brenda Wilding, Carol Conomos, Catherine Felix, Mary Herrold, Isobel Cunningham, Patricia Hercus, Rebecca Copeland, Lois Stewart, Adrienne R. Thrythal, and Jill Liddell, Tokyo. 1983. 83″ x 56″ (210 x 142 cm). *Yukata* cottons and Japanese sheeting. Hand-pieced, appliquéd, and quilted. This was the quilt that spawned a thousand others (well, nearly a hundred anyway!). In 1983, a group of us adapted *kamon* patterns and made this sampler quilt in *yukata* cottons, and the combination proved irresistible. Between 1983 and 1987, some seventy similar blue-and-white *kamon* quilts have been made as a souvenir of Japan, and there are more in the pipeline, with many of them being made by Japanese, who with their inimitable design sense have elaborated the *kamon* theme. Photograph courtesy Ben Simmons.

121. *Blue-and-White Kamon Quilt* by Miwako Kimura, Tokyo. 1986. 81″ x 54″ (207 x 137 cm). *Yukata* cottons and broadcloth. Hand-pieced, appliquéd, and quilted using a "quilt-as-you-go" technique. Ever since she visited a quilt exhibition in Chicago in 1980, Kimura yearned to make a quilt using traditional Japanese fabrics. Her dream finally became a reality in 1986 when she joined a foreign quiltmaking class. "I decided not to contrast the *yukata* with another color," she says, "but stick to a true Oriental blue-and-white color scheme." The ingenious way she has balanced the different tones and scales of pattern is a testimony to her designing skills (she trained as an interior designer). This was her first quilt, and it appeared on the cover of *Patchwork Quilt Tsūshin*, No. 13, and it has been exhibited in Tokyo on a number of occasions. She then made a small wholecloth quilt to improve her quilting skills, and moved on to her next work, which is the multipatterned masterpiece illustrated in figure 125. See also the extraordinarily beautiful piece called *Sakura* illustrated in figure 74 and on the front cover of this book.

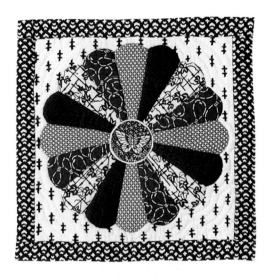

121a. *Chrysanthemum*. The stylized sixteen-petaled chrysanthemum has been the Japanese imperial crest since the thirteenth century, and has always been a popular decorative motif. The Japanese used this pattern on their porcelain, which was collected by the German prince who founded the Meissen factory in Dresden and who borrowed Japanese decorative designs. It is possible that the pattern reached America on Dresden porcelain and subsequently was adapted for the unusually popular Dresden Plate pattern. The Japanese often filled in each "petal" on their porcelain with patterns derived from textiles.

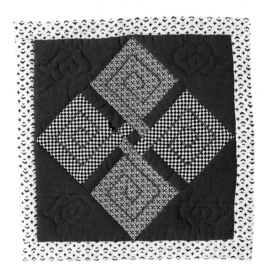

121b. *Lightning*. A family crest with martial implications, ideal for a samurai family. The motif derives from an ancient Chinese decorative pattern that probably came to Japan in the sixth century A.D., when the Japanese "borrowed" many political and cultural institutions from China.

121c. *Bamboo*. Bamboo has played a vitally important role in Japan since ancient times, and bamboo insignia were used as "carriage crests" in the thirteenth century. But the feeling the Japanese have for this plant far transcends its universality in art, architecture, and crafts. Its resilient strength and natural grace has moved poets and philosophers, and its phenomenal ability to flourish throughout the year has caused it to become a symbol of integrity and fortitude.

122. *Family Crest Quilt* by Sueko Murata, Kawasaki City, Kanagawa Prefecture. 1987. 94″ x 64″ (239 x 163 cm). *Yukata* cottons, Japanese sheeting. Hand-pieced, appliquéd, quilted, *sashiko*-quilted. Here is another Japanese quiltmaker who found the combination of *kamon* and *yukata* irresistible; this is her second quilt. She chose the elegant coloring to match her Victorian furniture. It is surprising how different these *kamon* quilts look in spite of their similar sampler setting. This is due to the fact that each quiltmaker is attracted by different *kamon* patterns. Included in this piece are a round Chinese fan, Mount Fuji, and a ship that Murata has set in a sea of swirling *sashiko*-stitched waves. Murata learned to quilt when she lived in Australia, and she is now a member of an international group in Tokyo, where she teaches others the tricks of combining *yukata* patterns of varying scales. She is one of the few young Japanese women who wear kimono regularly, and she graciously modeled the *yukata* for us in figure 119.

122a. *Mount Fuji.* Mount Fuji needs little introduction, for it, together with *geisha* and cherry blossoms, are the three icons that immediately evoke Japan in the minds of Westerners. Mountains represent the masculine *yang* force in the Chinese *yin-yang* cosmology and were therefore popular as a family crest. The stylized shape in the foreground is a symbol for water (the *yin* force), and Murata has outlined it with *sashiko* stitching. The background is a *yukata* fabric printed with a poem.

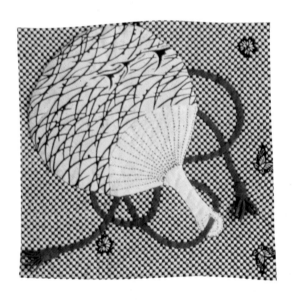

122b. *Round Fan.* The round fan originated in China (the Japanese invented the folding fan), and they are used in Japan during the summer. Paradoxically, they also have military associations and were therefore an auspicious family crest. Large round fans were carried into battle bearing the clan crest. Recently, summer fans have been printed with *yukata* patterns, so Murata has used this contemporary style in her attractive block.

122c. *Sailing Ship.* Ships like this used to ply the coastal waters of Japan, carrying goods from one part of the country to the other. Their sails would be ornamented with the crest of the owner. The seas can be rough in this part of the world, which Murata has cleverly reproduced with wonderful swirling *sashiko*-stitching: Ships are also important in Japanese folklore, for if you dream about a "treasure boat," you will become rich.

123. *Memories of Japan* by Adrienne Westmore, Falls Church, Virginia. 1985. 52″ x 52″ (132 x 132 cm). *Yukata* cottons, Japanese sheeting. Hand-appliquéd, embroidered, and quilted. For her striking *kamon* quilt, made as a souvenir of her stay in Tokyo, Westmore has chosen emblems that she has tried, whenever possible, to appliqué against *yukata* printed with the appropriate design. The fans at the lower left are backed by a fabric stenciled with scattered fans. Similarly, the design of red umbrellas next to it is complemented by a background densely printed with open parasols. *Yukata* prints share many of the patterns and motifs that appear in this heraldic source because *kamon* represent the basic elements of Japanese design. Like so many other foreigners, Westmore was attracted by the design possibilities of combining *kamon* and *yukata*, and she has elegantly spiced her "Japanese" quilt with a traditional Oriental red, using it both in the blocks and the binding. A quiltmaker of long-standing, Westmore has now returned to the United States.

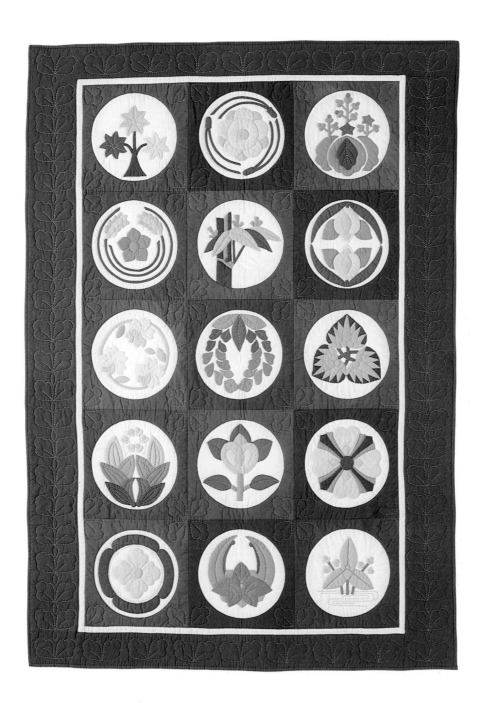

124. *Kagamon* by Sachiko Aragane, Kobe City, Hyogo Prefecture. 1983. 83″ x 57″ (210 x 146 cm). Hand-dyed cottons. Hand-appliquéd and *sashiko*-quilted. In 1983 when Sachiko Aragane made this beautiful quilt that has the clarity of Oriental enamel work, she was almost alone among Japanese quiltmakers in using *kamon* patterns. Although *kamon* are dyed on traditional clothing and depicted in the classic heraldic handbooks in monochrome, there was a time when colored crests were fashionable. During the long period (1639–1854) of Japan's isolation from the rest of the world, a fantasy world developed in the official "pleasure" districts of the major cities that parodied the stratified warrior society outside. Actors, courtesans, and brothel-keepers took crests as their personal trademark, and these were sometimes colored. These demimondaine crests were called *kagamon*, hence the title of this quilt. Aragane has chosen flower designs and tells us that the coloring of each block was inspired by traditional *kabuki* theatrical costumes. This exquisitely worked *kamon* quilt was hung in the first national exhibition of Japanese quilts, "Quilt in Japan," held in Tokyo in 1985. Aragane runs a large group in Kobe, and she has published two books.

125. *The Tide* by Miwako Kimura, Tokyo. 1986. 51″ x 67″ (130 x 170 cm). Old *aizome* and *kasuri* cottons, stenciled kimono lining. Hand-pieced, reverse-appliquéd, *sashiko-* and hand-quilted. The maker of this superb compendium of popular Japanese designs and traditional fabrics decided to combine everything she liked in this one quilt, using as many different quiltmaking techniques as she could. She chose natural phenomena as her theme and built her design around a beautifully worked family crest based on a wave, a symbol of power and resilience. She made each section of her multifaceted background separately, and then joined these to the central "wave." Each pattern in the background employs a different technique, and individual elements from these designs appear as family crests. Working clockwise from the top left: *kumo* ("clouds") was curve-pieced and ornamentally quilted; *inazuma* ("lightning") was done in reverse-appliqué and *sashiko*-quilted; *seigaiha* ("blue waves") was made with double clamshell patchwork; and the triangles, *uroko*, which represent "fishscales" in Japan, are patched. "As there was no living thing in my quilt," Kimura tells us, "I cut the cranes from the lining of an old cotton kimono and appliquéd them on last." Kimura made the striking *kamon* sampler quilt in figure 121. Photograph courtesy Ryuta Kimura.

126. *For Dear Bob Fujii* by Hiroko Kawahito, Kanonji City, Kagawa Prefecture. 1986. 80″ x 61″ (204 x 156 cm). Old *aizome* stenciled prints, resist-dyed cotton *futon* cover. Hand-pieced, appliquéd, and quilted. Here you can see how the Japanese used to display their family crest as the focal point on a *futon* cover. Kawahito's daughter spent some time in the United States with a Japanese-American family under a "home-stay" program, and Kawahito made this engaging quilt as a gift for her daughter's host. She honored both families by cutting out the Fujii family crest (a design based on a summer plant) and appliquéing it to another *futon* cover resist-dyed with cranes, for her family uses a crane as the logo for their sake-brewing business. (Another of her crane quilts is illustrated in figure 83.) "I had to introduce patchwork in order to disguise some tears in the *futon* cover," she says, "but breathing new life into these old fabrics and finding a way of disguising their injuries is part of the charm of quiltmaking for me." A third crane quilt was exhibited at the 1985 International Quilt Festival in Houston and was illustrated in *Hands All Around*. Shikoku Island, where the Kawahito family lives, used to be the main source of indigo dye and was an area rich in resist-dyed textiles.

127. *Late Autumn* by Nobuko Kamata, Osaka. 1986. 87" x 76" (220 x 194 cm). Japanese sheeting and cotton prints. Hand-pieced and quilted. Although Kamata took the pattern for this distinctively colored and superbly pieced quilt from an antique obi, it is a design that could well have been used by a member of the Japanese nobility in the eleventh century as a fabric design for clothing. The unusual coloring was chosen to reflect autumn. "I tried to convey a mountainside in the dying months of the year," says the quiltmaker. Kamata is somebody who evidently enjoys intricate piecework, for hexagons are not an easy pattern to put together. Be sure to notice how she has fashioned the narrow inner border of each hexagon. There are sixty-six, thin, one-inch triangles in each inner border. Kamata quilted the centers with a *kamon* based on the clover-shaped leaf of the wood sorrel. So many of these floral *kamon* have an interesting symbolism. Wood sorrel was highly esteemed by warrior families because of its remarkable fecundity (each plant produces masses of tiny seeds)— an auspicious portent for a family line! The border is quilted with an ancient stylized flower pattern that is often used in conjunction with hexagons. Kamata received an award from a house-decorating magazine for one of her other quilts. She is a student of Sachiko Aragane, whose superb *kamon* quilt is illustrated in figure 124.

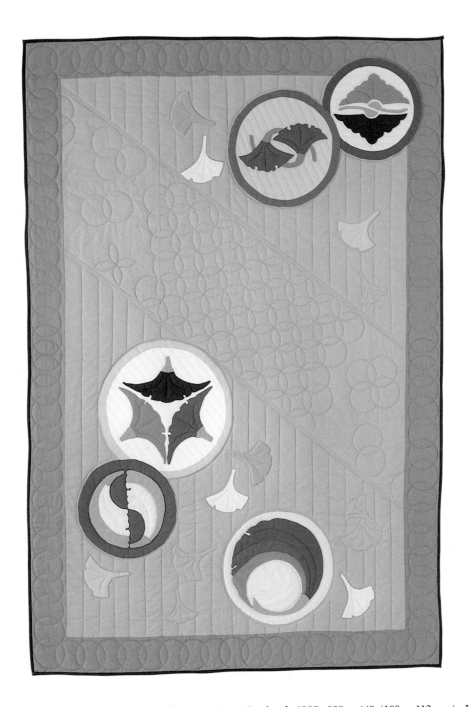

128. *Gingko Leaves* by Erica Main, Wellington, New Zealand. 1985. 63″ x 44″ (160 x 112 cm). Japanese sheeting. Hand-appliquéd and quilted. Main was living in Tokyo when she decided to try her hand at copying the well-known Japanese decorative device of scattered and overlapping medallion forms. She was one of the first quilters to do so. "The philosophy behind it was really: why need blocks be square," Main tells us. "I had always admired this irregular kind of Japanese design, and I thought it could be adapted for quilts and add a sense of movement that the standard sampler setting lacks." She chose for her patterns variations on the shape of the gingko leaf (an emblem associated with Tokyo), for like the Japanese she was enchanted by its wonderful yellow coloring in the early autumn. "I included some realistic gingko leaves too," Main adds, "because the *kamon* are so stylized as to be almost unrecognizable." Main first pieced each block as a square to avoid stretching the edges, and then cut them and appliquéd them to the background fabric. Her broken quilting design adds another touch of Japanese irregularity. The Mains have now returned to their native New Zealand, where Erica Main's *kamon* quilts have aroused much interest. She made three while she was in Tokyo, and her work was widely exhibited.

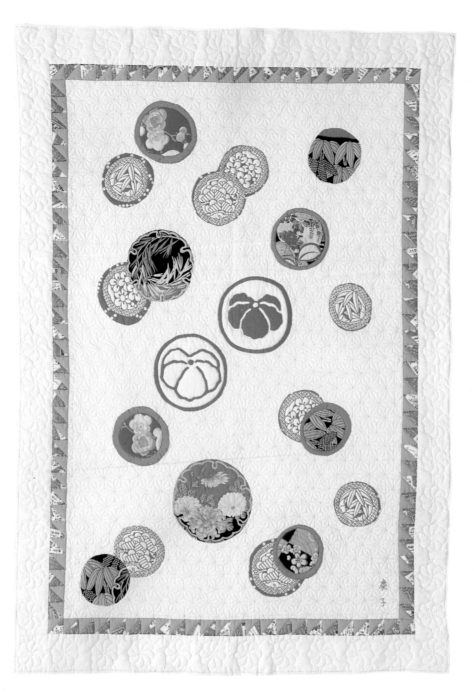

129. *Shochikubai* ("Pine, Bamboo, and Plum") by Keiko Nakamura, Tokyo. 1986. 63″ x 45″ (160 x 115 cm).
Cotton and kimono silks. Hand-appliquéd, hand-pieced, and quilted. Nakamura tells us that she was attracted
by the "floating block" *kamon* quilts made by foreigners in Japan and decided to make one herself. She says
she didn't feel competent to draw up the patterns, so for her charming quilt she cut medallion forms from a
stencil-dyed child's kimono and matching coat ("I'm not sure that all of them are completely round"). Most of
the medallions contained one or another of the flora of the quilt's title. *Shochikubai* is a felicitious pattern often
found on wedding kimono, for it symbolizes good fortune and fortitude because the pine and the bamboo,
both hardy trees, survive the winter with their leaves intact, while the plum blooms bravely in February, often
in the snow. The trio originally came from China, where they are eloquently known as "The Three
Companions of the Deep Cold." Nakamura also included her own family crest—the ivy leaf seen in positive
and negative forms in the center. Interestingly, when the Japanese assemble these randomly placed patterns,
it is the voids between the motifs that concern them most. If the width and depth of the voids prove
harmonious to the eye, then the designer does not bother too much about the relative weight and color of the
patterns—all of which is almost totally opposite to the approach of most Western quiltmakers. Nakamura
quilted her appealing *kamon* quilt with a well-known Japanese pattern that represents a hemp leaf.

130. *Furoshiki Kamon* by Keiko Saegusa, Koshigaya City, Saitama Prefecture. 1985. 41″ x 39″ (105 x 99 cm). Cotton *furoshiki* and *yukata* cottons. Hand-appliquéd and quilted. Keiko Saegusa had been using this *furoshiki*, resist-dyed with overlapping white crests, as a protective cover for her traditional wooden chest of drawers. She decided to turn it into a quilt after seeing some of the other medallion-*kamon* quilts. She had previously made a patchwork quilt from leftover pieces of *yukata*, and because her hometown is noted for its *yukata* production, she cut additional printed crests from some *yukata* cotton and also appliquéd them. She says that the background color of the *furoshiki* is typically *kabuki*, meaning that it is the kind of bright color used for stage costumes. For this reason she included an appliquéd pattern to the "nested measuring cup" crest of a famous line of *kabuki* actors (black-and-white motif at top left and also repeated in the quilting design). "When I see how the Americans used their lovely traditional patterns in their antique quilts, I felt it was high time that we Japanese began using ours." Saegusa is the organizer of a large quilt group.

131. *Kamon and Kimono* by Jill Liddell, Tokyo. 1987. 70″ x 46″ (178 x 117 cm). Cotton prints and solids. Machine-pieced, hand-appliquéd, and quilted by Chizuko Minematsu much better than I could have done. Japanese design uses a number of different outline shapes to enclose pattern elements; for example: hexagons, diamonds, circles, and fans, which are then scattered on textiles or painted on screens. It is an idea that I thought would be interesting to try—an extension of the "why need blocks be square" mentioned by Erica Main (see fig. 128). Every motif used in this quilt appears in the classic handbooks of family crests, even the checks and the quilting pattern. Checks became fashionable after a famous *kabuki* actor wore them as part of his stage costumes in the eighteenth century, and the quilting pattern is an ancient courtly design called *shippo*, or "seven treasures." The floral emblems are, of course, more orthodox *kamon*, and the quilt's theme is the "Four Seasons." (Cherry blossoms for spring, irises for summer, maples for autumn, and the check pattern for winter because an old name for this design—before it acquired the name of the *kabuki* actor—was *arare*, meaning "hailstones.") Having been brought up in the Western tradition of symmetry, I now find it unbearably dull because of my having lived in Japan for six years. Japanese design is a constant source of inspiration for me. The asymmetrical arrangement was copied from a seventeenth-century book of kimono designs.

132. *Encounter* by Margo Aldag, Tacoma, Washington. 1985. 50″ x 34″ (127 x 86 cm). Japanese sheeting. Hand-pieced, appliquéd, and quilted, machine-assembled. This American quiltmaker says that from the moment she first arrived in Japan in 1982 she was fascinated by the color and design sense of the Japanese ("it was evident everywhere I looked"), and like so many other foreigners she was particularly drawn to the stylized patterns of Japanese *kamon*. Born and raised in a historic quiltmaking area in Indiana, Aldag says she loves Amish coloring, "so I decided to combine these two diverse cultures in a quilt. I enjoyed the encounter!" Although culturally diverse in their ways of life, the Japanese and the Amish share characteristics that are discernible in this quilt. Black as a background color is common to both cultures and so is the virtue of thrift. Aldag's use of odd bits to frame each of her striking *kamon* blocks is illustrative of the Amish habit of "making-do" that creates the natural spontaneity their quilts have and which is also so evident in the Japanese quilts in this book. Although she had never made a quilt until she came to Tokyo, Aldag was inspired to start by the enthusiasm found among the Japanese for her native American craft.

133. *Memory of Grandma* by Eiko Furukawa, Kyoto. 1986. 54″ x 46″ (137 x 117 cm). Kimono cottons and solid cotton sheeting. Hand-pieced, appliquéd, and quilted. The brown, black, and gray-striped fabrics in this crisp contemporary-looking quilt are well over sixty years old, and the "Rail Fence" pattern, familiar to all American quiltmakers, appears in a dictionary of ancient Japanese designs. Furukawa chose it because she wanted to illustrate the universality of so many of these geometric patterns. The quilt is made in memory of her grandmother, for the "logs" of the fence are cut from one of her grandmother's kimono that she had inherited. When she finished the quilt, she offered it to the spirit of her grandmother at the family altar. "I sensed that it received her blessing," she says. The design for pieced blocks that are randomly scattered on the border is the crest of a famous line of *kabuki* actors, based on the nest of wooden boxes the Japanese use for standard measurement of grains and liquids and which has become an extremely popular pattern among quiltmakers here. This well-balanced and beautifully quilted work was Furukawa's second quilt. "It was like putting on a *furisode*—it was my 'coming-of-age.'" (A *furisode* is a kimono with a long dropped sleeve that young women traditionally wear at their coming-of-age ceremony at the age of twenty.)

133a. This woodblock print of 1807 by Toyokuni shows a *kabuki* actor wearing a costume with the famous "nest of measuring boxes" *kamon* on his sleeves. Photograph courtesy the Trustees of the Victoria and Albert Museum, London.

134. *Kimono Memory* by Marina S. Ratliff, Daly City, California. 1985. 89″ x 69″ (225 x 175 cm). Old kimono fabrics, *kasuri* cottons, solid blue cotton. Pieced and *sashiko*-quilted. "I visited Japan in 1985 with a group of quilters from the Santa Clara Valley Quilt Association, and when I returned I wanted to commemorate this dream vacation in a quilt," explains the American maker of this striking "Japanese" quilt. She bought most of her fabrics at flea markets while in Japan, but supplemented them with hand-dyed pieces of her own. A souvenir of the trip were some *kamon* patterns given to the group by Japanese quiltmakers, and, because Ratliff, like the others in her group, had become enamored with *sashiko*, she adapted these patterns for her beautifully worked alternative blocks. With all these souvenirs included in the quilt, the obvious name for it was *Kimono Memory,* and Ratliff tells us that "it has been *very* popular!" It was featured in *Quilt World;* was shown in the Editor's Choice section at the Houston Quilt Festival; won Third Place in the Capital City Quilt Show in Sacramento, California, in 1986; and was hung in the American Quilters' Society exhibition in 1987. The Santa Clara Valley Quilt Association used it on their poster for their Quilt Auction, and a copy of the quilt was sold at the auction. "The list goes on, so for once I guess I did something right!" she says with justifiable pride. Photograph courtesy the artist.

135. *Clove Medallion Quilt* by Yoko Nakajima, Fukui City, Fukui Prefecture. 1986. 64″ x 64″ (162 x 162 cm).
Antique *aizome* cottons, indigo-dyed cotton, cotton prints. Hand-pieced, appliquéd, and quilted. Cloves came
to Japan from Malacca in the tenth century, and they were prized by the imperial court for their scent and for
their medicinal properties and were also used as a crest by several leading families. This beautiful Medallion
quilt honors the humble clove in the magnificent indigo-dyed centerpiece. The clove motif was drawn on the
cloth by the *tsutsugaki* method, and the background was dyed by stencil—a decorative combination not often
seen. Nakajima cut the clove motif from the back of a kimono-shaped *futon* cover (*kaimaki*; see fig. 1). She
arranged her design so that it seemingly floats on a series of expanding borders, symbolizing the way that this
exotic spice spread to all parts of the world. She has contrasted the varied indigo blues with a subtly patterned
fabric that reminds us of some of the early Indian cottons and Indonesian batiks. We find in this quilt a true
marriage of East and West, and it is, therefore, a suitable candidate with which to finish our book. Quarter
sections of an American pattern (Georgetown Circle) guard the four corners, while borders of Wild Goose
Chase frame the areas quilted with traditional Japanese designs. The clove itself is curled in the mysterious
comma-shape that can be found in the decorative art of ancient Greece, Egypt, Basque Spain, China, Korea,
and Japan—a universal emblem that unites all nations and all quiltmakers everywhere.

Notes

1. Averil Colby, *Quilting* (London: B.T. Batsford Ltd., 1972), p. 18, quoting *Country Life Annual*, 1956, p. 168.

2. Li Xueqin, *Eastern Zhou and Qin Civilizations*, trans. by K. C. Chang. (New Haven and London: Yale University Press, 1985), pp. 363–64.

3. Marie Lyman, "Distant Mountains: The Influence of Funzo-e on the Tradition of Buddhist Clerical Robes in Japan." in *Festival of Fibers*, a companion handbook to the twenty-second lecture series organized by the College Women's Association of Japan 1988, p. 45; and abridged from an article in *Textile Museum Journal* (1984).

4. Ibid, p. 47.

5. There is also a *funzo-e* in the collection of The Metropolitan Museum of New York dating from the Edo period (1615–1867), but this one is a design of clouds and, according to Marie Lyman, the quilting is much coarser.

6. Penny McMorris, *Crazy Quilts* (New York: E. P. Dutton, 1984), p. 12.

7. Clara Whitney, *Clara's Diary; An American Girl in Meiji Japan*, edited by M. William Steele and Tamiko Ichimata (Tokyo and New York: Kondansha International Ltd., 1978).

8. Ibid, p. 79.

9. There are two books on Japanese *kamon* patterns that are available in the U.S. John W. Dower (with over 2,700 crests drawn by Kiyoshi Kawamoto), *The Elements of Japanese Design: A Handbook of Family Crests, Heraldry and Symbolism* (New York and Tokyo: John Weatherhill, 1971). *Japanese Design Motifs: Matsuya Piece-Goods Store* (New York: Dover Publications).

About the Authors

JILL LIDDELL learned American quiltmaking in Hong Kong when her husband, an international banker, was posted there in the early seventies. Since then, she says, it has become her passport. "Wherever you go in the world today, you find pockets of quilters who are stitching away and using the same techniques, the same terminology, and who are always welcoming to a newcomer." British by birth and a journalist by profession, Jill has traveled widely. The Liddells had lived in many parts of Africa, including South Africa and Kenya, and in Europe—France and Switzerland—before they moved to the Far East, where they spent six years in Japan—"the longest we have ever lived anywhere in our married life." Now they have returned to their native London, where Jill teaches and lectures on quilts. She has three children and five grandchildren, so she is also kept busy making quilts.

YUKO WATANABE was born in Yokohama, Japan, in 1949. She has worked with fashion-related magazines in Japan since 1968. As editor of *Patchwork Quilt Tsūshin* and *Patchwork Lesson* magazines, the largest and most successful quilting magazines in Japan, she has seen thousands of quilts made by various artists from every area of Japan. While working in various subjects related to fashion, Watanabe developed an interest in the cultures of Southeast Asia and lived in Bangkok, Thailand, from 1977 to 1979. She coauthored two guide books on Southeast Asia—the result of her travels through the countries surrounding Thailand, where she was studying the techniques and patterns of their textiles. Yuko Watanabe's other interests include ceramics and Baroque and Asian music, and she is an avid reader of literature. She is an expert on authentic Japanese cuisine and has coauthored a book on the subject.